Bible
Interpretations

Eighteenth Series
October 6 – December 29, 1895

Judges, Ruth, I Samuel, Isaiah, Luke

Bible Interpretations

Eighteenth Series

Judges, Ruth, I Samuel, Isaiah, Luke

These Bible Interpretations were published in the Inter-Ocean Newspaper in Chicago, Illinois during the late eighteen nineties.

By

Emma Curtis Hopkins

President of the Emma Curtis Hopkins Theological Seminary at Chicago, Illinois

WISEWOMAN PRESS

Bible Interpretations: Eighteenth Series

By Emma Curtis Hopkins

© WiseWoman Press 2014

Managing Editor: Michael Terranova

ISBN: 978-0945385-69-1

WiseWoman Press

Vancouver, WA 98665

www.wisewomanpress.com

www.emmacurtishopkins.com

CONTENTS

Editors Note

All lessons starting with the Seventh Series of Bible Interpretations will be Sunday postings from the Inter-Ocean Newspaper in Chicago, Illinois. Many of the lessons in the following series were retrieved from the International New Thought Association Archives, in Mesa, Arizona by, Rev Joanna Rogers. Many others were retrieved from libraries in Chicago, and the Library of Congress, by Rev. Natalie Jean.

All the lessons follow the Sunday School Lesson Plan published in "Peloubet's International Sunday School Lessons". The passages to be studied are selected by an International Committee of traditional Bible Scholars.

Some of the Emma's lessons don't have a title. In these cases the heading will say "Comments and Explanations of the Golden Text," followed by the Bible passages to be studied.

Foreword

By Rev. Natalie R. Jean

I have read many teachings by Emma Curtis Hopkins, but the teachings that touch the very essence of my soul are her Bible Interpretations. There are many books written on the teachings of the Bible, but none can touch the surface of the true messages more than these Bible interpretations. With each word you can feel and see how Spirit spoke through Emma. The mystical interpretations take you on a wonderful journey to Self Realization.

Each passage opens your consciousness to a new awareness of the realities of life. The illusions of life seem to disappear through each interpretation. Emma teaches that we are the key that unlocks the doorway to the light that shines within. She incorporates ideals of other religions into her teachings, in order to understand the commonalities, so that there is a complete understanding of our Oneness. Emma opens our eyes and mind to a better today and exciting future.

Emma Curtis Hopkins, one of the Founders of New Thought teaches us to love ourselves, to speak our Truth, and to focus on our Good. My life has moved in wonderful directions because of her teachings. I know the only thing that can move me in this world is God. May these interpretations guide you to a similar path and may you truly remember that "There Is Good For You and You Ought to Have It."

Introduction

Emma Curtis Hopkins was born in 1849 in Killingsly, Connecticut. She passed on April 8, 1925. Mrs. Hopkins had a marvelous education and could read many of the worlds classical texts in their original language. During her extensive studies she was always able to discover the Universal Truths in each of the world's sacred traditions. She quotes from many of these teachings in her writings. As she was a very private person, we know little about her personal life. What we do know has been gleaned from other people or from the archived writings we have been able to discover.

Emma Curtis Hopkins was one of the greatest influences on the New Thought movement in the United States. She taught over 50,000 people the Universal Truth of knowing "God is All there is." She taught many of founders of early New Thought, and in turn these individuals expanded the influence of her teachings. All of her writings encourage the student to enter into a personal relationship with God. She presses us to deny anything except the Truth of this spiritual Presence in every area of our lives. This is the central focus of all her teachings.

The first six series of Bible Interpretations were presented at her seminary in Chicago, Illinois. The remaining Series', probably close to thirty, were printed in the Inter Ocean Newspaper in Chicago. Many of the lessons are no longer available for various reasons. It is the intention of WiseWoman Press to publish as many of these Bible Interpretations as possible. Our hope is that any missing lessons will be found or directed to us.

I am very honored to join the long line of people that have been involved in publishing Emma Curtis Hopkins's Bible Interpretations. Some confusion exists as to the numbering sequence of the lessons. In the early 1920's many of the lessons were published by the Highwatch Fellowship. Inadvertently the first two lessons were omitted from the numbering system. Rev. Joanna Rogers has corrected this mistake by finding the first two lessons and restoring them to their rightful place in the order. Rev. Rogers has been able to find many of the missing lessons at the International New Thought Alliance archives in Mesa, Arizona. Rev. Rogers painstakingly scoured the archives for the missing lessons as well as for Mrs. Hopkins other works. She has published much of what was discovered. WiseWoman Press is now publishing the correctly numbered series of the Bible Interpretations.

In the early 1940's, there was a resurgence of interest in Emma's works. At that time, Highwatch Fellowship began to publish many of her writings, and it was then that *High Mysticism*, her seminal work was published. Previously, the material contained in High Mysticism was only available as individual lessons and was brought together in book form for the first time. Although there were many errors in these first publications and many Bible verses were incorrectly quoted, I am happy to announce that WiseWoman Press is now publishing *High Mysticism* in the a corrected format. This corrected form was scanned faithfully from the original, individual lessons.

The next person to publish some of the Bible Lessons was Rev. Marge Flotron from the Ministry of Truth International in Chicago, Illinois. She published the Bible Lessons as well as many of Emma's other works. By her initiative, Emma's writings were brought to a larger audience when DeVorss & Company, a longtime publisher of Truth Teachings, took on the publication of her key works.

In addition, Dr. Carmelita Trowbridge, founding minister of The Sanctuary of Truth in Alhambra, California, inspired her assistant minister, Rev. Shirley Lawrence, to publish many of Emma's works, including the first three series of Bible Interpretations. Rev. Lawrence created mail order courses for many of these Series. She has graciously passed on any information she had, in order to assure that these works continue to inspire individuals and groups who are called to further study of the teachings of Mrs. Hopkins.

Finally, a very special acknowledgement goes to Rev Natalie Jean, who has worked diligently to retrieve several of Emma's lessons from the Library of Congress, as well as libraries in Chicago. Rev. Jean hand-typed many of the lessons she found on microfilm. Much of what she found is on her website, www.highwatch.net.

It is with a grateful heart that I am able to pass on these wonderful teachings. I have been studying dear Emma's works for fifteen years. I was introduced to her writings by my mentor and teacher, Rev. Marcia Sutton. I have been overjoyed with the results of delving deeply into these Truth Teachings.

In 2004, I wrote a Sacred Covenant entitled "Resurrecting Emma," and created a website, www.emmacurtishopkins.com. The result of creating this covenant and website has brought many of Emma's works into my hands and has deepened my faith in God. As a result of my love for these works, I was led to become a member of Wise-Woman Press and to publish these wonderful teachings. God is Good.

My understanding of Truth from these divinely inspired teachings keeps bringing great Joy, Freedom, and Peace to my life.

Dear reader; It is with an open heart that I offer these works to you, and I know they will touch you as they have touched me. Together we are living in the Truth that God is truly present, and living for and through each of us.

The greatest Truth Emma presented to us is "My Good is my God, Omnipresent, Omnipotent and Omniscient."

Rev. Michael Terranova

WiseWoman Press

Vancouver, Washington, 2010

LESSON I

Missing

LESSON II

Gideon's Triumph

Judges 7:13-23

Last week's Bible lesson held up to the student's view the difference manifested by the congregated world, whether *in toto,* or by nations, when judged by brainy-headed leaders or by spiritually enlightened friends. It showed how Joshua, with his unflinching sight of loyalty in the faces of his soldiers and citizens, always fired them to loyalty. It showed how his unflinching sight of ability in them always brought out splendid ability. It showed how by always seeing them as cleaned by their own endeavors they came up to the mark in conduct and devoutness. The very instant his truly mother way of looking at the congregated world-child ceased and the Solomon style of mother-judgment began, the records report that the whole mass of people called Children of Israel did evil in the sight of the Lord and served Baalam. (Judges 2:11)

It hits our own age a sharp blow, because it seems pretty plain now that those who, see the world as a "bad lot" have the floor everywhere. These are very smart as teachers and lecturers and they keep our teeth chattering with terror as to what is coming next at the hands of the people of the world, as they read off their statistics of crime and shout tocsins for the imprisonment of all except themselves. That lesson made a full end of Joshua, the seer of the best and believer in the divinest in mankind. But as that does not touch the Joshua mind of this age it was not necessary to write about how the world was one too many for such a seer.

The Triumph Of Gideon

Today's lesson has for its subject the triumph of Gideon. Its golden text reads: "Though a host should encamp against about me, my heart shall not fail." The texts may be found in Judges 7:13-23.

It touches the greatest chord in the heart of the world, and the mutest chord. It speaks to that in the heart which, when open, leaps up, and makes the heart glad and courageous. Gideon, of Israel (1222 B.C.) defeated an army of war-like Midianites, numbering 135,000, with a company of 300 men of the peaceable families of ancient Jewry. He had his eye on the eternally finished kingdom that rests here in our midst, and this pulled its strings of assistance.

How long Gideon has been watching it of the fifty years of his quiet life there is no telling, but we remember that Jesus watched it thirty years before it identified itself so with him that he was it, and Moses spent forty years before he could rally force of its irresistible quality enough to take the Jews out of Egypt. Even then he did not get enough identified with it so that he could find Canaan. This Gideon had encouraging promptings, by the way, like Bruce with his spider, Washington with his vision. Columbus with his voice. A soldier in the ranks dreamed that a cake of barley fell on a Midianitish tent and it tumbled to pieces. The barley cake represented the army of Gideon, as compared with that of his foes. He took this dream of the soldier, and spoke all his words from that moment on the side of the victory of his men. This was different from Napoleon, who was always calculating what he should do in the case of defeat.

On the subject, Jesus was explicit when speaking to all this world, whose affairs follow the heels of their words: "Sit thou on the right hand till I make thine enemies thy footstool." It did not apply to himself after his identification with the supreme, for then his word forms did not manufacture anything for him. It was what he was in himself that counted all. Truth is not something that is already so related to things for the Jesus Christ man; it is what he makes it. If he chooses to have five plus nine equal one hundred, or less, it will be found that he is right, but Gideon and Napoleon were not identified with the Supreme Original so finely as that. Their words and thoughts counted.

What Christian Science Does

The Christian Science that is explainable deals with that plane of life where Gideon and Napoleon dwelt. It harangues all the time about how, by our words and thoughts we are teased or honored in life. Gideon never struck a star higher than language and action, and so his victory should be often read over by the talkers about truth.

The mighty "Something" which can charge statements with energy is not explainable. Even the expression which Jesus used is a mystery: "Watch." Emerson was sometimes hissed for talking about keeping his eye on the Eternal. The Bhagavad-Gita calls this watch of the Eternal in this unexplainable fashion the Supreme Secret to Know. If it were not that Gideon's words turned around into destiny and managed everything so promptly, we should think he had spent all his life repeating truth with his lips while his eyes were on temporal affairs, for he demanded so many signs before he would proceed in the power of his Lord. The Jesus Christ man demands no signs. With his eye on the Supreme, let it manage its own affairs; what is this to him? To him the Supreme One is visible in all affairs of small or large. This is really the only miracle-working part for us to take, whether we like it or not. Note the Oriental Bible on this point: "Whoever, undeluded, worships Me in all forms, Knows Me as everywhere supreme. Thus has this most secret instruction now been declared by me. Knowing this, a man becomes the doer of all that is to be done."

The story of Gideon points out the comforting fact that attention to the Everlasting One is certain to endow a man with life in himself.

Dante has spoken slightly of the stars which shine with self-derivative energy. Swedenborg has spoken harshly of men who live from themselves, but Jesus lived the mighty fact that as the Father hath life in himself, so hath he given the Son to have life in himself.

Whosoever sees the Self-sufficient One, some day sees that himself is self-sufficient. Whoever watches the Self-energizing One some day finds himself a self-energizing efficiency. Gideon had seen the self-inspiring and self- empowering one long enough, so that he realized self-inspiration and self- empowering. Nobody ever does any healing service except as he sees a self-acting principle performing near him. Jesus taught this Gideon lesson in a few words: "The son can do nothing, only what he seeth the Father doing," People talk about the self-feeding power of jealousy; how the more we talk of what has fed the jealous streak with us, detailing now our loved ones have given other people more attention than they have given us, we get more and more jealous, till we become perfectly unbearable. Even so, this shady-side of

7

mind hints at the sunny splendor of the day, when though father and mother depart, there is the Lord Eternal; though lover and friend fade away, there is the Lord Eternal. Who is all this, and much more; though all the fates are against us, there is the Lord Eternal, master of fates; and as we see the master of fate and ordainer of what shall be truth, we see that we are also handlers of fate; we see that with us also it is true that what we say is true — is true and what we say is not true — is not true, and this makes it easy, easy as the spreading of milky ways on the horns of the robes of endless skies, to defeat a world with the talents we now have on hand, boiled down to their minimum of incompetency; which is all the Gideon's successful encounter of three hundred to one hundred and thirty-five thousand ever meant for any student of the mysteries of his own life, its purpose, and destiny.

Bible Lesson October 13, 1895

LESSON III

The Divine Ego

Ruth 1:4-22

Last Sunday's Bible lesson (printed in Monday's issue of the Inter Ocean) had for its subject the triumph of the divine ego in man, when pitted against a whole phalanx of the worst possible human disadvantaged. It was an inspiration to fearlessness. It taught the unpreached principle of self-derivative life and energy.

It showed how great a mistake it is to teach ourselves that we have a limited storage of strength; for the truth is that one touch of the divine ego that rests so still within us is capable of making us drawers of unending forces from within ourselves. "As the Father hath life in himself even so hath he given the son to have life in himself." "I set before you an open door, which no man can shut."

Ibsen is popular as an author for setting it down with such a Norwegian need that man is a

9

limited being. This may be very interesting for the intellect to ponder over, but it is not Jesus Christ.

Almost every man, woman, and child has been incrusted with some of the idea of limitation but the new interpretations of the everlasting Bible texts will take off that crust and set the spreading streams and beams of the unendable energy going on their free courses from the heart wells of all the people.

Let us before him, become familiar with the new interpretations.

This lesson is to be found in Ruth, chapter 1, 4-22. Ruth was not endable. She was the eternal ego in humanity. The name means "Rose of Moab." No end to its perfume. Orpah was the intellectual ego in humanity. Ruskin and Emerson stand out on the pages of living pictures as showing how certain Orpah is to wind up. Only the divine ego is with us eternally. We cannot get rid of the divine ego. We may entreat Naomi, but entreaties affect it not! We may be widowed and old and penniless and friendless, but the ever young, ever beautiful, ever sublime Ruth, rose with wondrous perfumes to scent the moldy years of ages on ages with language and gesture matchless in grace, is still there.

The Lesson Taught by Ruth

Ruth was a contemporary of Gideon, and therefore she was well chosen, as the subject of this lesson, for she carried out in multiples what Gideon proclaimed as one.

She had all against her in the hand-to-hand fight with destiny exactly as he had, but she showed how easy it is for the ego that dieth not and fainteth not to shine on and shine forth till it can stand in glory on an earth as the God-strong Jesus Christ. Ruth was the great-grandmother of King David and the sweetly fair ancestress of Jesus.

She knew the value of Naomi and her religion through the rags of poverty and the wrinkles of tears. This penetrating vision, seeing through the most uncomely of veils the majesty of the great man or woman in our midst, is evidence of our own greatness.

Cadijah is known as the maker of Mohammed through steadfast recognition of his native powers. Rahab, the harlot, became the far-off ancestress of Jesus through steadfast recognition of the Jews as sons of God, while yet her neighbors all said they were fiends. England has the honor of recognizing Walt Whitman while Americans looked askance.

"For prejudice that spider shrewd,
    Did o'er them weave in wicked mood,
Threads of slander, threads of shame."

The greatness of Queen Elizabeth consisted in knowing ability when she saw it, and loves and fears, her own or somebody else's never caused her to finish from seeing what she saw. It is a great thing to look straight through our own eyes, through the cobwebs of slander and the films of praise.

The Shame of Being Led by Others

This is the shame of those sniveling audiences that sit listening to ministerial descriptions of the depravity of humanity. They see through the speaker's eyes, and that is the only cause that ever could possibly exist for finally having to wear spectacles. Everybody who wears spectacles sees people as somebody he loves or hates sees them. When he sees straight from his Ruth ego or the unentreatable exactness of his own judgment, he will throw down his specs and his eyes will shine like the Mithra fires, beacon lights of a secret flame of increasing wisdom.

Though the suns of the distant skies shall grow cold and dematerialize, though the stars shall sink in final faintness behind a horizon visible only to the cherubim of Paradise, still shall the divine Ruth in man, the divine ego, be saying: "Entreat me not to leave thee, or return from following after thee; for wither thou goest I will go; and where thou lodgest I will lodge; thou people shall be my people, and thy God my God; where thou diest will I die, and there will I be buried."

Oh! Well for the boy whose mother, like Pope's shall see him great through the hunchbacking of other men's and women's estimates! Oh! Well for the broken-hearted traveler over the long desert marches of human existence if somebody sees his majesty and mightiness. For the boy will honor his country and his maker, and the traveler will pick up his courage and do better than he dreamed. Every man should have his Cadijah; every woman should have her Ruth. History does not tell much about any man ever having recognized the possibilities of life for a soul that peered through the veilings of decrepit and weeping old womanhood, but Ruth felt with the sun-tipped fingers of divine foresight the coming motherhood of kings through cleaving to Naomi, who while companioned by earthly advantages was worth something to Orpah, the intellect, but failing in these fell away from her forever.

Foregleams of the Visions of Time

Through the secret doctrines of the new interpretations we have here in this chapter the foregleam of the last visions of time. It tells how the tenement of the clay is not despicable, but transfigurable. Naomi stands for the tenement of clay. She thinks she must part company from both intellect and soul, but as Naomi could only get rid of Orpah, so even the form of man and woman can never be separated from the divine ego, the soul.

Though the wrap of coats of years and tears surround us, still shine within us the flaming splendor of Ruth, our deathless faintless beautiful soul. Though we hang down our broken heads on the dry stalks of his appointed days and nights, there, in our bosom, sings Ruth, rose of eternal morning.

Whosoever leaneth his tired head on the Ruth keepeth him company shall rise up refreshed and bring forth kingly deeds for his offspring. Whosoever has a Cadijah to tell him how matchless is his strength it is well, but whosoever recognizes himself for himself without a friend or a helper, while slanders and misfortunes pelt thick and fast, he has laid his head on the changeless bosom of his own eternal soul, and his majesty and inspiration, his strength, and his beauty shall transfigure his very shape of clay till, as Ruth foregleamed Jesus at the mystery of transfiguration, so every man, woman, child, may transfigure himself by hearing the voice of his own Ruth. What shall it profit a man if he gain the whole world of objects, but cannot throw through them the beams of his own soul?

Inter-Ocean Newspaper, October 20, 1895
     * This is how Emma puts the comparison in her *Twelve Powers of the Soul.*

"This is the Jesus Christ in you. It is sometimes called the divine ego in you, sometimes called the divine soul of you, sometimes your deathless, changeless spirit."

Inter-Ocean Newspaper, October 21, 1895

LESSON IV

All Is Good

I Samuel 3:1-11

There is a science of mind which is very interesting. There are schools for teaching this science. They explain conscious and unconscious cerebration. All men, and even animals, live or die by cerebration. In the conventional schools they are reluctantly admitting that thoughts may make disease or cure it, but in the unconventional they positively aver it. In these latter schools they prove that thoughts held secretly are either health breeders or disease breeders. Then they select some thoughts for some people to think for three years or so, till their unconscious cerebration gets its machinery running their way. These thoughts which are thus select they call their religion.

Today's lesson shows the straight outcome of one of these thoughts as it was held by Eli, a Jew, 1212 to 1120 years B.C. He said "All is good." If a man stole the temple money, he said: "All is good." If one of his own sons did the same thing he said:

15

"All is good." He had trained himself to affirm; he had not trained himself to deny. It sounds very plausible and flattering to the universe to affirm that all is good, no matter what miserable tale is rehearsed, but it is not the Jesus Christ science for in that "if any man will come after me let him deny" the evidences of his senses and the educations of his mind.

The effect upon Eli was enervating. His manliness was sapped. There was never a robust; reliable character, yet who kept on averring "all is good," when its bold proclamation should have been: There is no reality to evil; no power in it whatsoever." These lessons are all faithful illustrations of the principles held by the characters.

Moses believed himself to be good, but his people to be bad. This kept him going often into retirements to revive himself from his encounters with them. Joshua believed they had been cleansed for their badness, and now had clean hearts and faces. Naomi believed that her spiritual power and her intellectual acumen must both depart from her when she had become disheveled by tears and years. This belief was quite able to dispose of her intellect — Orpah — but she was the everlasting declaration that the souls that are in this shape of clay never can be put away by conscious or unconscious cerebration, for Ruth, her soul fire, said firmly: "I will not return from following after thee." Ruth was the undeniable soul. No state of mind can alter the soul fire burning in eternal youth and splendor just behind all people.

Face to Face with the Unalterable.

All the schools that show how diseases can be brought on by the thoughts and throw off by thoughts are spending their time for nought save to amuse themselves, for they are dealing with the alterable. This lesson is brought up to show that it is the part of the good judgment to deal hand to hand and face to face with the unalterable. It is written out to show that if a man says stealing and lying are good he is making a reality of them and praising them up. It is meant to explain unto us that there is a fine difference between saying adultery and cheating are good, and saying: "I deny their existence or their power." One way breeds them, the other dissolves them.

This lesson is recorded on the pages of life to show that on the plane of cerebration, where disease and tobacco chewing are built up by thoughts and dissolved by thoughts, we shall always find that we can build up good eyes or break them down by trained mental actions, but there is a subtle flame of smiling intelligence and beauty which no way of thinking can build up or tear down.

Samuel stands in this lesson for one who knew this soul flame. Such a one, from his noble mountain height of un-assailable wisdom, knowing the mind, and its exploits; also he knows material manifestations and what produce them, but he is not identified with either. (I Samuel, 3:1-11)

It is mental science, here called Eli, which brings Samuel into view, because if one steps along in mental science as far and fast as it will take him, not tying himself to the apron strings of some so-called teacher, he will soon see that his heart's desire is for something which is not contemptibly dependent on his words and thoughts for its nature and office. This very desire points the way, and Samuel is found ministering. Samuel means "Asked of God."

Denying Evil Means Dissolving It

The two sons of Eli are brought forth just far enough in this lesson to show the effect of praising up the power of evil thinking, thereby to lessen it, when denying its power is the one way to dissolve it.

The principal of denial is entirely necessary if the principle of affirmation is practiced. They are pairs of opposites forever engaged in hand to hand friendship hewing out a straight path for the uncontaminated one to come walking in. They are the cloven tongue that mows down and sets up. They are the swinging sword that keeps the way clear. Eli had only used one and so had got sideways. Samuel explained this to him. To Eli's honor let it be said, he understood it.

He also understood that it was too much of an undertaking to handle his mind any more with the effort to manage his affairs by it. He saw that it was far better to turn his gaze toward the unmanageable I Am burning with the living ability at his God center and keep watching it till it had settled his affairs its own way.

He understood that the watch of his I Am flame which Samuel represented would attend to all things better than he could ask or even think. All in an instant it came to him that he had spent all his time attending to his religion instead of his God.

Faithful to Religion, False to His God

He had been faithful to his religion, but it was perfectly merciless in its exactness. "All is good" had come to its ripeness, and tasted terribly bitter. So he bowed his head and stopped religioning forever but kept watch of his God.

"Behold the Lamb of God, that taketh away the sins of the world." Eli had nothing to do with the consequences. He turned his back on his whole past life and mind. So the great neutral wrought dissolution and rebuilding. Eli rested. "Behold, I make all things new." Not Eli, with thoughts or speech or hands making over new conditions, but the great I Am.

The science of mind is wearisome beyond tolling, though practiced on the heights of fine thoughts, calculated, mold and shape conditions into fine states. The science of the unmanageable soul is restful. There is no thinking mixed up in its almighty executiveness. There are no actions mixed up with its almighty achievements. That

19

which constitutes this science is the immaculate concept.

Steadfast and Immaculate

The gaze of man at the smokeless fire of his own-starting point, the ever accompanying I Am that first started him out on his journey. Look unto me and ye be saved, all ye ends of action and ends of mind. Let your steadfast gaze be immaculate of descriptions of me, for I am not that which you describe.

Let your steadfast gaze be immaculate of actions, for my works upon the earth need none of your efforts. This lesson teaches that the universe will run in unimpeachable perfectness if we are not trying to help it. This lesson teaches that acquaintance with the I Am that sent us forth is only accomplished by watching it. Then it speaks with a voice. Then it spreads our table before us. Then it clothes and shelters us. Then it empowers us with powers the like of which are not now upon the earth. The day spring from on high visiteth us. There is a direct perception of the Samuel or Soul. After about ten thousand years of repeating the name Brahm the Orientals, jaded to almost as thread bare nothingness as Eli, have said: "Liberation is not possible by the pronunciation of the word Brahm, but only by direct perception of the Supreme.

Inter-Ocean Newspaper, October 27, 1895

LESSON V

If Thine Eye Be Single

I Samuel 7:5-12

The theme involved in this lesson is the value of unmixed motive in the principle of success. If one is a "health-food" student he can never really determine about safe and unsafe victuals if he takes spasmodic spells of practicing the Christian doctrine of eating whatsoever is set before us and asking no questions. If one is a believer this minute in liniments and massage and the next minute in the unformulated spirit, how can he expect to arrive at successful health? If one is watching for astral shapes, karma, reincarnation, and so on, how can he mix his vision with the High and Holy One and find out anything definite?

"If thine eye be single the whole body shall be full of light." But if the light in thee be no stronger than what angels can tell thee thy whole body shall be full of an inferior light.

21

Samuel, as was said last Sunday, represents one whose mystic gaze is always fixed on the highest. This illuminates him to see what is less and estimate it at its proper value instantly. He learned of metaphysics how to face the Best, and he never compromised on something less. Eli represented the metaphysics which has got far enough to say words over and over with the key information to them that the words formulate affairs and bodies. Samuel took the key and spoke the highest word he had ever heard. It was "Lord". Whoever says "Lord" much hears a voice.

"Thou shalt hear a voice behind thee."

Listening to the voice turns the mystic gaze backward and upward. No spirit of just men made perfect or astral shapes, or angels after that, can be heard by him without his detecting at once that his "Lord's" voice is more reliable and buoying. He knows the values of words and sentences, and yet he never studied them. So little Samuel knew, as last Sunday's lesson rehearsed, that cheating and opium eating like to be told that they are good instead of being denied any reality.

He told that to Eli and Eli immediately let go practicing making his world spin around by right words. He saw that it would never get right for he could never get power from words. His power must come from that which is above words. Samuel is here represented as having parted company with the doctrine of language altogether. He takes his whole realm of body, mind, feelings, spirit, and turns them into the bottomless pit of the majestic and mighty "Lord," within him. (I Samuel 7:5)

He Who Prays Shall Be Victor

"Mispah" is only figurative for high watch tower. Which is the highest within. It was to turn all his "Israel" into his "Lord" that should constitute success. The Lord is often called "He" in the Bible. "He will swallow up death in victory, and the rebuke of his people shall he take away." Nothing is able to swallow up death and hell and satan and the mind that imagined them except that "He" who is mentioned in the Bible. It was unto this capable swallower that Samuel turned his undivided attention. All prayer is attention to that "He" who can swallow up sorrow, danger, death, fear. Mary, Queen of Scots, said she feared John Knox's prayers more than an army of 10,000 men. You had better look out how you speak of the man or woman who prays much. Also look out how you deal with them. They are always victorious, triumphant, successful.

All Israel gathered and poured water in the ground together, to signify that the past was nothing — nothing at all. Whatever Samuel was saying was all they knew anything about. This was unmixed motive, undivided attention. (verse 6) The Philistines saw this congregation losing itself in Samuel's judgment, and fell upon them to destroy him. So at first, whatever science or principle, or object you give your attention to, all your old ideas, feelings, beliefs, all the people you know, and all the affairs you ever had any dealings with, will come up to distract you. Philistines are only distractions.

Distractions are either nothing or something to you, according to how well lost you are in Samuel. This, of course, means only interest, or intentness. Some people are not half interested in what they are doing. They are not interested in the God they are talking about. How can you tell? Why, they complain of this, of that, of the other. If they were really interested, do you think, they would know what was going on around them?

At a boarding school the students complained of the severity of the professor of mathematics. One of the boys was so interested in the mathematics itself that he never once caught the sarcasms, the quick-tempered reproofs of his teacher. That which was the teacher's goal was his goal also. No Philistines distracted him. Lorenzo Dow was on his way to a meeting, where he was to tell of the glory of God. His horse kicked and plunged and suddenly balked, throwing him violently ahead in the road, Dow got up on his feet and went on as though nothing had happened. He never even looked around see where the horse was, and he never inquired what became of him.

"Here I'll raise my Ebenezer.
    Hither by thy help I'm come;
And I hope by thy good pleasure,
    Safely to arrive at home."

24

Jesus Took the World with Him

This lesson is wholly taken up with the actual presence of something in our midst which is of such entrancing ability that we are glad to commit our life, destiny, reputation, body, and affairs into its capable fingers. Samuel is the quality in us which; by some luminous elixir, can pull the whole of our faculties into itself. And the Samuel of us, in us, never asks help or expects help, except from one source, (verse 12), "Hitherto hath the Lord helped us."

You cannot tell whether your eyesight would be glory, straight gift from the mighty God, can you, if you are pulling on your spectacles all the time for your sight? You cannot tell, can you, whether your robust body would be your glory, straight gift from the mighty God, if you are pulling at the drug bottle all the time for your health?

Now there is a Samuel faculty in us which can pull on the mighty I Am till death, blindness, disease, danger, yea, even our very flesh and mind are drawn into its vortex and nothing is left of us, but "he that shall rebuke the devourer for our sakes."

Jesus of Nazareth took his whole being and offered it into the great void of that which swallows all, leaving itself the only presence to be found anywhere. He took all the world with him and offered everything in it and on it along with himself. Samuel only took David — that is, all who

25

had heard of his God. Jesus took those that never knew there was a God. His pull on the earth as he offers it to his own I Am is still very great. It is even more felt than it was a year ago, for the time of the loss of the old heaven and the new earth into the open gate is closing.

Every knee shall bow and every tongue shall confess; the ministry of Jesus shall be complete, and he shall give up the keys to the Father. Give up his drawing powers, his name; the rulership contained in his name. The new name shall take his name's place.

In verse 9, it tells how Samuel took a little lamb and burned it alive. This is but symbolic. If anybody slay a little lamb, even for food, he would be doing something for which he could hardly pray himself from the consequences of. The law is so strict as it sweeps its inflexible winds over humanity that it is as certain as you live that even for the deed of cutting off a horse's tail there is to come a pain exactly like it in the body of the man who did it. For every blow on an animal there is to be a blow exactly like it on the quivering skin of the man who strikes. This is law. And the very fact that a man is capable of doing these things marks him plainly as one under the law of cause and consequence.

Therefore, whether Samuel, judge of Israel, 1114 B.C., or myself, 1895 A.D., it is one and the same if we set our murderous purpose on a living animal. We shall not pass one jot or one tittle till

26

all be fulfilled in us. In the Jesus Christ freedom, there is no instantaneous release from these consequences, to be sure, but while there is any practice of hurt in our life we have never actually accepted the Jesus Christ. We are only half way interested. We have not even got as far as Samuel and Israel.

The Story of Cruelty but a Figure

So, the story of cruelty is only a figure. The lamb that Israel offered just represents our most blameless doctrine. Now, the most blameless doctrine ever presented to man is that the spirit in man is his identical substance with the absolute God. This is full of sweet meat, full of warm comfort, full of gentle healing. It is the lamb dogma that is lifted up for glad humanity to accept just at the closing whirls of the cycles of time. Matter has been called a real substance. It has been studied and believed in till mankind is now the faintest live shape that moves. He is the sickest. He is the most afraid. He is the most foolish. Of all these states produced by studying matter, the sweet dogma that spirit is the omnipresent substance is sure cure. The man who finds that spiritis the strength of his life and the light of his countenance will rally from a deathbed and renew the intelligence of his youth.

It is a doctrine which has clothed the ragged and given courage to the famine stricken. But Jesus said the poor in spirit touch God. The spirit in man, even at its most shining glory of power and beauty, is not the hallowed Father. Ye must be shed of spirit-poor-devoid. No spirit lives on when you touch the I Am, Father, nameless God.

Now, this lesson shows that it is a fire, a burning flame that is experienced when man lays down his precious healing spirit. He feels a new fire. As a man who has eaten no food feels a burning so a man who has given up his dogma that his spirit is God, indeed, feels flame. But who hath known the smokeless fire if yielding up his lamb doctrine that at his pristine point, the original Shen as it is called in verse 12, he is spirit?

No he is not spirit. He sheds spirit as a radiance forth from his nameless center and all the nations cry: "Beautiful spirit! Wonderful God!" But on the untouched pinnacle of his mighty self he is that of which the spirit can know nothing. This is what burning the lamb means.

Legend of the Mystic Mountain

The Mohammedans tell this story of giving up all to the Lily that is nameless in a better symbol than this Samuel lesson tells it. They say there is a mystic mountain of fire, and whenever a ship is sailing toward it the nails, the spars, the shrouds, the very flames, begin to feel the pull of the mystic flames and flee from the ship toward it as toward their longed-for haven. So there is soon nothing left of the ship, but the splendid mountain stands in eternal calm, with the enchanting draughting energy which all who sail its way cannot resist.

"As the thirsty hart panteth after the water brooks so panteth my soul after thee, O God!"

Samuel is described by commentators as one who had to struggle like a man to hold himself against the temptation of the degenerate social life of his age. But the divinest teaching that the mystic fire from the mountain of my God has given me is that he whose eye is on the eternal never fights for his life, his chaste character, or his conduct. He never struggles. He never makes effort.

As he gazes on the father in heaven a noble character rises up in him, which he did not win by feeling every fiber of his body and mind quiver to do some sensual thing and finally mastering it by some great struggle. This is old- fashioned understanding of the majesty and ability of the soul. It is no effort for the God of heaven to be holy, mighty, wise, and it is no effort for any man who sails the ship of his undivided attention toward the shining mountain of the living I Am, that has its throne in his own bosom, to be holy, strong, blameless, capable.

There are other things than keeping the character blameless and the actions grand, which the new sweetness of the drawing flame of the fire mountain shows us do indeed take place as we draw near the hour, from whence no traveler returns, but as this lesson is about Samuel with his blameless and competent manhood, some other lesson must tell of those other glad miracles.

Inter-Ocean Newspaper, November 3, 1895

LESSON VI

Saul Chosen King

I Samuel 10:17-27

The section of Bible history best picturing the changes taking place this week in the silent place where governments are founded is I Sam.10:17-27. The subject is "Saul chosen King". The golden text is "The Lord reigneth; let the earth rejoice."

The story is of the Jews of B.C.1095. The Jews always represent hope. They are always looking forward. Every movement they make, they hope for another one, and all movements are looking forward to the golden age of a perfect king who is coming.

Plato looked forward. Socrates looked forward. Seekers after truth look forward. But they all have that for which they are waiting hidden near them, exactly as this chapter says. Saul, the son of Kish, was "hidden among the stuff" doctrines of futurity. (Verse 22)

Plato and Socrates and the Jews all knew that all that really is cannot be here any more than it already is. They all knew that all that we want is right at hand, and always has been here. The pyramids are a mere second in age by the side of the age of that that our hands can touch with its molecules covering our own possessions.

Knowing this, it is singular how much they all cast their eyes forward and outward, blearing and weakening the sight thereof all the time, when they ought to have stayed at home on their own base and found what they wanted under their feet.

In each man's lot, he really has within the network of his business affairs one golden spring to press, and there will be exposed a kindly stroke to help him. It was help, help, help the Jews wanted, powerful help. They believed themselves to be in great trouble. They looked behind the business duds, and there was Saul. Standing straight up, the lithe lad towered head and shoulders higher than any man amongst them. (Verse 23)

This is only figurative. The helping hand just at our shoulders is stronger and larger than any other hand in range. The head that is planning for our assistance this moment, unpretentiously, secretly, is entirely capable, no matter who derides that head and hand. (Verse 27)

Always take home to yourself the Bible sections chosen by the International Religious Board for Sunday's meditation. If you will thoroughly understand your own relation to the omnipotent center of power, you will understand the nation's progress, the world's progress and the state of religion and philosophy.

To Understand Self the First Requisite

Understanding of self is first. That sheds a light on the universe. This lesson teaches that we have been doing better latterly in striking toward what we want than ever before. We have been letting go of some blinding principles of every one of us, and the helping principle is plainer to us.

We are quick-witted enough to know the helping hand when it offers and the capable head when it proposes more certainly than we've been since we lighted on this globe. "God save the king." (Verse 24)

If we have had for a motto that "time and tide wait for no man," we brush the old axiom aside for a more helpful one. There is one that finally is to rule with a rod of iron. It erases time. It stops tides. We know it is the final — the absolute — the moment we hear it spoken.

It came out on the third round of Christian dogma, when it was found that a word had no power in itself, only such as we gave to it, any more than a poppy head has any power only what we give it. It was found that the power is vested in the "I" resident in every man. This is the man child that rules all nations with a rod of iron as has been prophesied.

The magnetic pole of the earth towards its iron base, the draw of the sun towards its magnetic center of irresistible iron, is symbolic of the irresistible pull of the doctrine of the "God I" in man.

"I if I be lifted up, will draw all men unto me." They all come swiftly to this offspring of the Kish of science. "Kish" was the father of Saul. The doctrine of the eternality of all that father really is fathers the I Am. The doctrine that "all is spirit, all is life, all is good, there is no matter, there is no death, there is no evil," drew all hurting power out of matter. That was the spiritual dogma that mothered the rise of the "I" with its entrancing elixirs when called Jesus Christ.

"Saul" is but a letter's hiding from soul. And the soul in man is his everlasting and unkillable "I". Let it be acknowledged as able to stand and fight for us, to stand and reach for us, to stand and draw for us. This is its stopless efficiency. It is well enough to expect a principle we have proclaimed to work as it reads, but the principle will not work if we draw its power out of it while the "I Am" — the "soul" — will work and nothing can hinder and nothing can deliver out of its hand when we turn its way.

Man's Strength and Energy

The principle, "time and tide wait for no man" is a dead letter when we know that our soul — the "I" of our being — can set time and tides aside or instigate them at its pleasure. So receiving Saul, son of Kish, was the same as receiving a principle with alterations in it suitable to decrees; but receiving Soul unalterable authority, world without end is the final. Whosoever receives the final stands up in his authority.

Whosoever receives a principle or aphorism gets what he can do in all its full as the Jews got Saul, a good king to fight the Ammonites.

"He that receiveth a prophet in the name of a prophet shall receive a prophet's reward." So he that receiveth a motto, an axiom, in the name of anaxiom, shall receive an axiom's reward. So he that receiveth the Almighty One in his own name shall be Almighty and that will be only what has always been, showing it forth in plain view. The historic sketches of scripture show up the empowering energy resident in numbers of people gathered together. The Jews always energized tall and stalwart men with great powers exactly as the wise men of India empower and energize that little boy of twelve years and then withdraw it from him to prod up another victim after a time.

The Persians energized Xerxes. As time went on, men grew weary of energizing tall and thick boned men and infused their forces into nervy men. Napoleon was small but nervy. The Apostle Paul was a little lame specimen but nervy. Isaac Watts3 was diminutive. Many other noted men had been insignificant in size but undaunted of nerve.

Using up the Rags and Fag Ends

Now, as the principle that all men were born of equal rights is gaining, some hold, we notice that it is customary to make presidents and governors out of the merest rags and fag ends of men; also kings and princes likewise, and they do just as will as any others to hang the fashions on and expose how little men are now interested in other men being made great, but they all want to be great themselves. This is a good sign. Each man to his hearthstone! Each man to his home! Each man to his native majesty! Each man to his own authority! Each man the seizure of his own kingdom! At his point of authority he is himself all that the multitudes use to empower a high-headed stripling with each generation.

Today let genius know that a powerful ally is here. Let the hard-pushed people know that somebody is lying low like Saul under the blankets and boxes of far-away Zuph, near Bethlehem, who will show what can be done with finance and inventions; capable of showing the present men in authority, who have left the people to fight the long years out by themselves and legislated not one line for their benefit.

He will rouse up like a lion, head and shoulders higher in knowledge and ways and means than all who are now making themselves ridiculous, more nervy than Napoleon, more guarded than Lincoln. This lesson says that the people demand him, that he is here.

Wishes of Men about to be Fulfilled

This lesson says that what each man has been wanting in the way of power is right at his hand now. It says that whoever knows enough to let axioms and doctrines and external operations alone and turn around to face himself will be doing best of all, yet this Bible section is meant as much for the encouragement of others as for him.

The axioms, the business affairs, the school books on hand are the "stuff" which being brushed aside, left behind, exposed the King in his glory.

"Why cry ye aloud? Is there no King in thee? Is thy councilor perished? called Micah. So there is a kingly helper for all people, always near at hand, always full of power, always all power.

The long brow-beaten inventor with one of the Astor's for his patrons, just now buying up all the stock in his patent, is but a definite signal set flying to show what is now here for all the world.

The very words for which the Christian board opens this lesson, stands for the way things are going today. Though their minds are set on the pages of antiquity, the words are of today; "we are now on the verge of a new era of government, a new development".

They do not know the principle that is taught in simple metaphysics, namely, that the words that the eyes are now watching are the conquering factors later on. Watch the word "friends" and draw an army of them. Watch the word "health" and draw an unlimited supply of it. Watch the word "now" and culminate all affairs promptly. Watch the I Am and be. Watch the I know and be wise. Watch the I Am empowered and rise up in new vigor. Watch the Jesus Christ and within this is all the fullness of the Godhead bodily, ruling all nations with a rod of iron.

The name of the unconquerable kinship invested in each is in this name. It is impartial in its effect when noticed. The poorest the most ignorant stand equal chances with the richest in receiving its rousing radiance.

Inter-Ocean Newspaper, November 10, 1895

LESSON VII

Saul Rejected

I Samuel 15:10-23

Today's lesson illustrates the principle of infusing with power and withdrawing power; that ability inherent and normal within our-soul-as-all, whereby we charge up poppy-heads with stupefying energy or refuse them energy at all according to our decrees.

Last Sunday it was mentioned that the Jews had a habit in most ancient times of investing tall and large-boned men with so much confidence that they could fight like heroes. Ahasuerus was thus invested by the Persians though he had no native intelligence whatever except that deeply hidden spirit, common to all creatures.

Here in this section, Sam. 15:10-23, we have Saul's fictitious power withdrawn from him and he is left to stand on his own merits.

We all know how soon he wilted after Samuel ceased inflating him with his share of praise and faith. How he even lost his mind and wandered around hunting David in jealous blindness instead of standing to his guns like a self- empowering individual with as good a right to the spirit of majesty as Samuel!

This lesson strikes us, as it were, a final rap to call our attention to ourselves. We are easily great and dignified and authoritative while people look upon us as so noble, so apart, so rich, so majestic, but when they withdraw their admiration, where are we? Do we cringe and falter and lose heart and mind? Then, of course, our greatness is only superimposed. It never sprang from the unquenchable fountain within.

It is like Saul's and like Xerxes!

There is a school in New York where they teach that we are all like slates upon which pictures have been made and if we are sick it is important to find the image on the mind slate which made that sickness, erase it, and draw another image which will make us well. Up to a certain point, this slate business works well, but, like all other manipulative operations, it reaches its limit because the mental slate is apt to wear out, and there is nobody yet found able to manufacture new mental slates.

The greatest illustration of the slate practice is the child of India, whose mental plate the wisdom men make *tabula rasa* (blank state) and then print upon it all they themselves know, thereby making a marvelous prodigy of information. But that little slate only lasts about twelve years. The wisdom men then withdraw all their interest in the child and he droops into nowhere.

If the child could be touched at his central "I am", or rather if those mystic-eyed sages could expose through the mysterious material of human shape, that deathless, independent originally first ego of that boy instead of painting him over with what they believe they would have the true system of education.

The Word Education Defined

"Education" is a wonderful word. It means drawing forth or exposing what is already there. It has been the wonderment of philosophers that so few school-bred men or deeply learned men have ever amounted to anything, and there is a question up now why our college-trained women seldom become famous. This lesson of Saul devitalized and the ever-recurring picture of the Child of India wilted, make it plain. Learning is but a handsome collection of photographs on the sensitized plate called human mind, while education is the exposure of original wisdom.

It is certain that there is as yet no system of bringing out the first glory of the child like the formula of Christian science, even if its practice has been known heretofore, chiefly, as washing off foolish notions that produce diseases. As we proceed in it we find that we have other foolish notions washed off, such as made us cowardly, for instance, or dependent upon our neighbors or family for our happiness, or our strength, or our self-esteem. We, by accepting it are like sleeping lions that rouse up, that stand high, that see anew.

This Saul lesson of today ought to please the religious minds of this age right well, because there is so much misery and punishment and despair in it. Saul, it seems, was more indebted to Samuel for the inflation of his mental cuticle than to the whole body of Jews combined. This is true of all the artificially empowered. There is one vigorous believer whose energy is more bolstering than the whole of the rest. A speaker who depends upon his audiences for his eloquence would certainly find that if that particular one in the audience should withdraw his or her favor, there would be as a sudden drop in his enthusiasm. Only those speakers are great who are fired by their theme and wholly unsusceptible to favor or famine of favor. As a younger man gets to understanding his audiences better, his identification with his theme gets less close. The government is on the shoulders of his audience, not on his. That day his candle flame dims. *"Solruit etmontes umbra.ntu"*. (The sun descends and the mountains are shadowed.)

Saul was not solicitous of being inflated to kingship by a combined confidence of the Jews. He even hid behind a pile of blankets and timber to get out of their way. But they compelled him. So that little boy of India is said to be the very picture of sadness because not permitted through all his earthly sojourn to be anything but a puff ball like

Saul or a slate like so many of us. He cannot be himself for even a minute of time.

Samuel was a wisdom man; a positive quality. When he infused Saul he was capable. Now, Saul did not know that except he were energized by Samuel he would collapse, any more than Napoleon knew that unfused by Josephine he would go by the board, so, when Samuel delayed coming to burn the sheep and oxen for incense to Jehovah, this Saul went to burning animals on his own account. Anybody whose greatness is super-imposed had better take care not to get out of favor with the chief imposer, for there is no pull from the unfailing Divine that he knows anything about while he is so dependent, and his fall is apt to be hard like Saul's, Xerxes' and Napoleon's.

All Blame Placed on the Invisible

Samuel saw that nobody should burn animals and draw down divine energy but himself. He was very positive, very persistent, very devoutly certain that the Absolute and Eternal God meant only him for such business, and all this, together, made him a powerful photographer. He not only withdrew his own favor from Saul, but he told him savagely and sorrowfully that the omnipotent goodness itself had withdrawn its favor also. He went further. He lashed him and spurned him, brow-beat him into inability to confess that he had tried one little sling of his big arms outward toward independent action.

Samuel said that the Lord Jehovah, Impartial Love, repented having let the people swell Saul into kingship. This only meant that the strong-minded, strong-willed, Samuel, was surprised that Saul was wearing out as a puff ball, or slate for images, or whatever other figure of speech best suits this particular case of illustration of man existence. The reason this section of Bible story ought to please the modern religionist is because both the commentaries and the context itself from Verse 10-23, inclusive, lay out poor Saul as an example of the way the great manager of this world flays human beings for disobeying what the ministers and priests tell them is wanted of them. It foists all the blame onto the invisible one.

Man can do all things with and for himself that he pleases, but only one honorable thing for his neighbor, and that is, give him his freedom. Take off the images, photographs, stories, from the col-lodion veil of childhood and let us hear what they have to tell. We have all been told that we were born to trouble and death. But what did we know of, before ever pre-historic man told that tale to the airs? What powers had we before teachers and parents told us we knew nothing and could do nothing? Is there not something that we are in ourselves which makes us worthwhile, even when our friends have fallen away, our allays are dead, our riches gone? Must we faint because some man or some woman, some army or lame church has stopped breathing their breath through our bodies

or wills? What can we be more than a community
of puff balls dependent upon some strong breath
from no telling where. If we go up in honor like
Saul with Samuel's favor and down in loss even of
common intelligence like Saul with Samuel's favor
withdrawn? Which is most important, to know
who our terrible Samuel is, or who we are at some
head center immovable by our Samuel?

Has anybody from India or Persia or Egypt exposed any boy who has never heard any tales
except of the glory that he had with the Father
before the world was? Has anybody from Chaldea
or Arabia or Ceylon ever shown us a boy who
would have none of our stories of the original
wickedness and incompetency of the sons of men?
Has any country ever produced a child who feared
not the fires or the floods or the swords or the
crosses devised by all the combined Samuels of all
times? Has any glorious face ever looked upon
mankind with smiling repose of security from being marked over with earth's favor or blame, just
as grand and inspiring when deserted by man as
when honored by man.

Obedience Is Better Than Sacrifice

If there has been such an one there can be others. If one has declined to come down or go up, to
enlarge or decrease by armies and nation's decrees, every child on this earth can decline the
game and go free as himself at his first estate.

Samuel spoke some splendid principles when
he was in his state of exalted indignation. In Verse

22 we find: "To obey is better than sacrifice, and to hearken than the fat of rams". He meant obey what he said. But what he said was only his rendering of the original message. To obey is to be what we were in the beginning before ever the words had reached us that there are miseries to defeat favors to win. The world says we can be powerful and efficient only as we have its acknowledgments. But to go in with that assertion even when a Samuel says so is not the obedience of the Jesus Christ type. He obeys his first self. It has ways of providing for him, and ways of instructing him all its own. And who shall say that his seamless coat and eternal eloquence were lacking in any way.

He has ways of coming and going that never the sound of an axe or hammer of hired labor made possible. He had ways of inspiring the hearts and lips with speech while never a word is escaping his lips, while never a soldier or sailor or pilot or Samuel befriends him.

Unfriended, yet dear as the breath of the everlasting God. Unassisted, yet swaying the dead in their graves with life pulses. Unhoused, yet every home hears the tread of his welcome feet and weeps with famished joy at the touch of his hand on the latch. All because he obeyed not man even at his Samuel declarations but obeyed himself.

His hearkening is his knowledge. His knowledge is not of how guns are made to defeat armies, not of how animals are slain to defeat soldiers, not of how machines are made to weave clothes, not of how to buy and sell, to govern and punish, but knowledge of his divine self. This is rich life. Samuel had it right. "Hearken unto the voice of the Lord in thy garden place." How tender and gentle!

Hearken again: "The Lord shall roar out of Zion." Hearken again: "The earth is filled with the knowledge of the Lord, as waters fill sea basins." Hearken again: "the language of earth has changed. For what a man hears first from himself, he hears secondly from his world."

The Jesus Christ in man, with his whip of soft soundless cords is driving again the money changers out of the temple. The whole earth is the temple this time. Galilee of old is enlarged to a planet. Jerusalem, the golden, has ceased to be a shining spot of antiquity. She hath risen through the aqueducts and spires of all the earth. For the people, who do know they are divine there must be Divine surroundings.

Inter-Ocean Newspaper, November 17, 1895

LESSON VIII

Temperence

Isaiah 5:11

This Sunday's section of Bible wisely follows last Sunday's. It tells of the power we have to energize inert matter with qualities or refuse it any qualities at all. Last Sunday Saul of Israel and Dalai Lama of India were exhibited as good illustrations of how well men act when praised and how willed they are when ignored. Today wine and rum are exhibited to illustrate how powerful they can get when praised but nothing is said about how impotent they are when de-energized.

Jesus once took water — simple, non-intoxicating water, and infused it with color and stimulating fire, to show how subservient to the authoritative king in man is all material substance.

He said to humanity: "Woman, what have I do to with thee?" He said to matter: "Matter, what hast thou to do with me? Get thee behind, into the

49

servant's place." He saw that his mother represented the highest type of dominion over man and
he declined to obey matter. He himself went free.
Matter obeyed him at every turn. He did not stop
at dissolving cataracts. He dissolved hunger and
un-happiness.

Schlatter, the Denver healer, has to stop at
bodily cures. They are the acme of his power, but
Jesus cured of hard want and world despair. There
are thousands of people in the United States who
can go in where strong-minded men with diplomas
have seen sickness and they will take this same
Jesus position about matter, and where the doc-
tors said there was power in material disease they
will refuse power, and there will be health where
there seemed first to be sickness, at their dicta-
tion. So it was but a step in the committee's minds
from devitalizing Saul to devitalizing rum; but
they did not know it. The lesson of November 10th
showed how pompous and competent Saul became
with praise. It did not allude to how wilted and
crazy he became with withdrawal of praise. So
today's lesson shows how pompous and competent
fermented drinks can get when talked of as powerful, but nothing is said of how wilted and insipid
they can get by withdrawal of praise. The committee praise up strong drink very eloquently. They
quote scripture to prove their assertions. We can
quote scripture for any premise and seem to prove
our position by it.

Let us expect that next week the lesson may rally to the Jesus Christ statements on those matters. "They shall drink any deadly thing and it shall not hurt them," etc. Let us hope that next Sunday's text may recall his demonstrations over matter and not exhibiting flinchings under matter like todays. Rum is God, or the other one, according to what a human being knows of himself first. If it draws and tempts and winks at him with suction pulls it is given power by him. If it seems to him as if it drew and sucked at boys with great energy he is investing it with government. The man who warns against the power of opium is as far from his own dominion over it as at the man who eats it and maunders.

Authoritative Head Center in Man

The Jesus Christ proposition from first to last is that there is an authoritative head center in man to speak from. The Jesus Christ scheme was to show man his authoritative head center in the quickest possible way. Nothing dare assert itself in the presence of the authoritative man. He is at his God base. It is most certain that poppy heads could not stupefy God. And it is most certain that at his base point man is God. The whole business of Jesus of Nazareth was to find his own base point first and other men's base point next.

All men have a purpose, motive, or scheme of life. Jesus had one. It was to find and act from his God center. There is no doubt, but he found and acted from it. In his scheme there was no power

51

given to matter. No power given to evils of any sort. They were subject to orders every time. Learned men have had their day with disputing Jesus perpetually. The sun of a new age gleams somewhere in the east of this age, when things do as we tell them; we don't do as they tell us. But no amount of bolstering up with illustrations and believers in us will enable us to prove it. We find that things require watching, and talking to, day and night when we are not managing them from the central authority vested in us. We have to work like dray horses with formulas while we are prodded up by teachers in these things. It is not till we are on the home base that we find the yoke easy, and the burden light.

It is a great task to insist that a shaking palsy isn't shaking while simply agreeing with some teacher's correct premises to that effect. It is no task at all when seeing from the self-convicted standpoint. The teacher says there is no lameness. We agree with the statement. The man disagrees. His family backs him up. We work our thoughts faithfully. So does he. So do his family. We finally win.

But there is another way of managing lameness than reasoning with the lame man's mind. It is by knowing our own Jesus Christ nature that we had before lameness was ever talked of. That is an easy way of curing. It is as easy to stop the power of opium as to stop the clutch of disease from that standpoint. Now, witness the years our smart men and women have been working at charging up fermented liquors with fictitious abilities. See what a short time the reasoners of the metaphysical order have been proclaiming that these liquors have no power only what we say they have, and that their severe clutch on man is only a false estimate. They truly have nothing in themselves one way or the other.

Jesus understood this perfectly. Moses understood it to some extent. Elisha understood it pretty well. Paul had got quite a ways in authority over matter. Schlatter touched the key note, but he carries the notion that he must have spells of starving himself faint before he can use it. There are many that can cure as well as Schlatter, who eat three times per day, and sleep like Jesus on a pillow. Does not this show that "the devils are subject," not masters? Even the matter of eating to his use of his native authority.

Man Makes His Own Matter or Slave

Catarrh rages or disappears according to what you use of your authority. Faintness does the same. Heart disease and dyspepsia come or go according to your use of your own authority. Poverty arrives or goes according to your dealing with it. Business thrives or fails according to your use of your own authority. Crops increase or diminish according to your use of your own authority. Matter is subject, slave, servant, or King, Alcohol, Governor, Opium, Prince Poverty, whichsoever you make it.

Just listen to Isaiah 5:11: "Woe unto them that follow strong drink." Of course. To follow is to us no authority at all. See the Orientals, with their abject slaves just behind. There are said to be princes and presidents who keep servants following them to watch out for assassins. Every man who sees opium as a governor is following it as much as the one who sees it as a drowning principle for his cares. This is a principle which the new age just shining in upon us will notice and prove.

Isaiah was sawn asunder in a hollow carob tree. He and Jeremiah believed profoundly in the governorship of matter over man. They studied along that line continually. They had superb formulating energies and used them for what? To declare that man at his unmanageable center was greater and stronger than strong drinks? No; that strong drinks would certainly cause honorable men to famish and multitudes to dry up like dead leaves.

It is heresy to all the reformers' and pious men's lingo, but it is gospel truth that not a piece of matter has any potentiality, only what is given it by man. It cannot poison or inflame or sicken, only according to the use of authority in that direction. It is Isaiah at this formulating machinery that we are studying today. He was a fine, firm, strong character, and he put out some of his splendid energies into coming man, to tell us that about this time there should some people arise who would not judge after the sight of the eyes, nor after the hearing of the ears, but entirely to suit themselves. And their judgment should be right judgment, and it should stand.

Somewhere about another period there should be a terrible decline of men. They should be blear-eyed by the millions, feeble-witted by the nations on all account of his infusing wine with so much kingliness. He did not tell his neighbors that he himself would be to blame for all this besotted-ness, but those who see what a vigorous infuser he was can see it plainly.

Then there never rose anybody to declare that serpents could only sting if we authorized them to sting, and poisons could only work if we authorized them to work, till about 800 years after Isaiah's time. The Jews were obedient to Isaiah's orders to all that time. They are not yet quite out from under his yoke, for many of them go reeling under the governship of that same stuff, exactly as Isaiah said they would, to this day.

Matter is the Ruling Power

This lesson is woe to man because matter is master over him. Let man flee — run — escape for his life — for matter is king. So, poor, inert, non-capable matter has it all its own. It tumbles to pieces, it falls down, it hurts, it pleases, it defiles, or cleanses according to what Adam named it; but Jesus Christ declined every single proposition of Isaiah on the overpowering vengeance of matter, and every single proposition of Adam as to its relations to man. We also have his ability to decline

55

the power of matter, and we can exercise it according to Jesus, or say let it reign in company with Isaiah.

It is a question of our use of our native authority. The name of that authority is the "I Am." The way to use it perfectly is to give it attention. It does not ask praise. It does not ask honor. It is indifferent to our blame. All it asks is attention. "My son, attend unto me." Even speaking foolishly to it counts with new authority for nothing we call wise speech is descriptive of it, and all our high sounding phrases shoot wide of the mark of telling what it is. This was illustrated by a blind man's looking up to the sky and saying. "I am not blind," with all his attention focused on himself. Suddenly his eye burst open and he could see. It is to the shame of Isaiah's splendid energies that he turned them into descriptions of outward managers over coming man, instead of turning them toward his own I AM and proclaiming that all men to come on this planet should know and nothing should forevermore have dominion over them, because they should know their dominion over all things.

Lovers of the World Its Martyrs

He flung forward his woes by the barrel. "Woe unto them that call evil good." The truth is that there is no evil only as we name it. How can we call it good, if it has no entity? "Woe unto them that put darkness for light," he says, in same verse. Then it is no wonder he himself caught the woe he shouted about. For is it not darkness to tell me that I am weaker than arsenic, if it is not true? "Woe unto them that put bitter for sweet," he said. And truly he was doing it himself, and the bitter carob tree loomed up before him.

But he also said that it should be woe to them that should put sweet and light and good into men's lives. And so it has gone on for many years that those who have tried to do the best they could for the world have been the martyrs, till now, when these explanations of how the Isaiahs and Jeremiahs and Ezekiels, and so forth energized negative sides if life with powers capable of lasting several generations, we find the new preachers go free from the effects of anathema and legislation.

Good religionists want to be loyal to Isaiah and keep rum in as president and governor and King over man, just as he said it was, and so they try to stop these heretical principles, but the new views are winning thousands upon thousands into their ranks.

There is a spirit in man and that spirit is his authority over matter. He can find that spirit in himself by attention to it. He can see that it is that spirit within him which is his wisdom. He can see that its true name is not spirit. He can see that no man knoweth its name. He feels that there is a great change taking place in his outward body as he gets more closely acquainted with his own spirit.

Man No Longer Mesmerized

He sees that outward events and business movements touch him at no point as they used to touch him. They slide out of his heart life. He begins to stand up and care very little what other men think of him. He cares very little what is happening around him. He finds that his own spirit, which is the only interesting thing about him, is able to set him into safe places, happy places, masterful places, and he is surprised to notice that it has done this for him, while he was acquainting himself with it. He understands Isaiah and is sorry, so far as that emotion can move him that so grand a force as he was should have talked if woes and famishings and faintings, instead of concerning the immortal and unmanageable ego, seated in all people. He is not mesmerized by Isaiah nor by Isaiah's coadjutors, who are this day descanting the praises of alcohol and opium. It is a great thing to get free from Isaiah's whizzing airtops, kept so bravely spinning by our great scholars and preachers. But it can be done.

"For the God in David still
    Guides the people at his will."

And the people that do know the God shall not fear, though the old earth be removed and the mountains be carried into the midst of the seas. It is their wish that the mountainous, monstrous doctrine of the power of matter over man should pass away. They wish the former ways of earth to cease. They are glad to stand up and see the land not pasted over with Isaiah's ideas.

Inter-Ocean Newspaper, November 24, 1895

LESSON IX

The Lord Looketh Upon The Heart

I Samuel 16:1-13

This lesson of I Samuel 16:1-13, touches upon the fifth lesson in metaphysical healing as arranged by Moses in the Book of Genesis, repeated by Esdras. It teaches getting as near nothing as we can get in order that we may be ourselves. Taken as we now roam in and out among our daily affairs, we are a set of photographs of other people's imprint and nobody knows how we would be and how we would act if we had the photographs washed off.

The effect of this Bible section is subtly soluble. The keynote of the fifth lesson is briefly put into a sentence thus: "The less there is of me, the greater I am, and the nearer nothing I am, the more I accomplish. Take as illustrations sleep and rest. Sleep is nothing —nothing — yet its working efficiency is incalculable. Rest is nothing — nothing

— yet if a man were as rested as God; he would work the works of God.

Descartes discovered that he was plastered over with teacher's wisdoms, so he sat still to see if he could not dissolve them. Think of a college president of today or a professor of anatomy, or of bacteria, willing to let go of his precious knowledge of bones and worms!

It is an unthinkable proposition. Yet the splendor of their reputation of which they are most jealous depends at this time upon their rejection of what they have learned. The study of this Bible section, without foisting upon it any preconceived notions will let them down gently. But it will certainly affect their memory badly for after a while they will be astounded, they have forgotten the name of an ear bone or a worm with a thousand eyes, or some other vital item in modern schooling.

To the wide-eyed metaphysician this would be a sign of quickening intelligence, but to the materialist it would be a sign of faltering brain. It truly would only mean that this lesson had begun its dissolving ministry. So, if anybody's bread and butter is dependent upon his memory of bugs and snakes, or linguistic idioms, he had better not know much about David's young life and Samuel's finding him in Ramah, and nothing whatsoever about Bethlehem, where he was anointed, and where the prince of peace was born, for the very names thereof are dememorizing, let alone a careful attention toward them which might denude even of interest in coleoptera and aorta carbuncles and cataracts; yea, even of bread and butter itself.

Lesson Which Jesus of Nazareth Loved

This day's lesson is, therefore, a dematerializing lesson. If one pursues it to the ultimate, it is a dementalizing lesson, also, for it can even stop the play of thoughts over the filmy globe of native mind.

Jesus of Nazareth loved this lesson. "He made himself of non-account." "In his humiliation, his judgment was taken away." "He answered nothing." "He that would save his life must lose it." "The son can do nothing." "It is not I that speak."

The golden text is the seventh verse: "Man looketh upon the outward appearance, but the Lord looketh upon the heart." The Lord-vision is a cleanser of photographs. Samuel had fixed up one king by the photographic process and it had failed. He mourned himself nearly sick over the failure of his Saul king, and this mourning made him meek. It took off a good share of his projective mind. It got him still. It washed his inward eyes, so that they would look Lord- fashion. He was thus capable discerning a youth who was nearer his own self than his seven brothers. (Verse 12)

Jesus of Nazareth could see gold in a fish. He could see beauty in a leper. He could see sight in the glued eye-balls. Outward appearances were nothing; original facts were all. Samuel saw seven young men who could be bolstered up by praise and withered by withdrawal of praise exactly like

Saul; but he was now looking for a youth who could keep himself intact. David was that youth; "Beloved one." Who does not love his own independence? Who does not lament his loss of independence? David was so free from other people's pictured thoughts that whatever anybody was looking for they could find in him as one who sees his own face in a free mirror. The father saw him as a keeper of sheep. The mother saw him as her baby. The brothers saw him as a little drudge. Samuel saw a king.

He stood so near himself that the strains of heavenly choirs chanted in living rhythms through all the reedy pasture lands and the hilly winds. He was so near himself that his voice sang angels' cadence over mountaintops of times to come. He was so near himself that his face was sun-smitten from the fadeless beauty of the nameless mother-God. He stood so near his native self that kings in after ages have paled into shades of kings and descended through the sanded floors of nowhere when compared with him — for they have been walking photographic collections of learned acquiescence; but he was himself as he was in the beginning, is now and ever shall be. Boy in the pastures of Bethlehem the ancient, close to the heart of the Infinite Mother, prefiguring the day when we, too, shall step back into our refuse of untaught majesty — king and father of kings!

Bethlehem was such a little place, and David was so young, and his mother was so insignificant that even her name was forgotten. And Samuel was so meek that he could not have any opinion of his own, and he was so old that the Jews could not write their wishes upon the sensitized film of his useless mind any more, and the seven stalwart men who could have pinched his slender frame between a thumb and finger could not impress him!

The State Without Contagion

But at the low-tide mark of man's ability, the finger of God sets the tongue to supernal speech and turns the hands to miracles that live as ever-lasting pointers heavenward, eternal monuments to the Divine One in our midst. Arise and anoint David! "For this is he." And the hands of dried up and drooping Samuel touched David. Think of being so near nothing, even while the marks of years are on our faces and in our hands that we can touch the original self that belongs to us. He anointed David. And to this day whoever knows that at his neutral center he is manager of destiny, he also touches David, and sees with Lord-vision that it is not forever that he shall be pushed into a corner, misrepresented and unjustly defrauded. He sees his own coming hour of stately independence.

The Scripture sections should always be applied to the Most High Self seated on the throne of each one of us. Seeing its ever-lasting presence is turning away from the seven stalwart pictures now printed on our minds and thus denying them.

The second lesson of healing metaphysics always talks of denials, rejections, refusals. Naaman washed seven times. Seven devils fled from Mary. Seven sons fell out of Samuel's vision. Seven stories told us since Adam spoke of an opposite to good to be let go of by our seeing David and touching David and hearing David sing of Paradise.

For the beloved state is the un-contagioned state. The key of David is meekness, simplicity, nothingness. Jesus had the key. Elisha often felt it. Abraham Lincoln had one hand on that key from cabin home to White House honors. He who yields up all that he hath and knows, and clings to, and turns to touch the unknown and undescribable King whom his Bible once called David, and lastly called Jesus, will rest from the swirls of the world. He will be near enough nothing so that he may be king, and forgotten enough so that he can do great works. Who is willing to be forgotten? Who is glad to be nothing? Who smiles at being rejected? Who stays where he can no longer learn anything? He is near David. The nearer nothing Samuel got, the nearer David became. And the nearer David became by the bitter road of disappointments in life, the nearer the fresh new life of a new line of kings he got.

So, this lesson takes Bethlehem, little place, and Samuel, worn out priest, and David, mother's young one, and mother, too near nothing to have a name, and teaches a lesson in the goodness of the

Eternal Presence which asks us not to do so much, that we are worthy, but to do nothing.

"Oh, to be Nothing, Nothing"

Asks us not to be so bustling and hustling and vigorous that we may be glorified for our works' sake, but to be nothing that in the glory of that shining Presence may be our glory, and in the mighty works of that Wonderful One, we are wonderful workers enough. It teaches that God forbid that I should boast save in Christ Jesus — bond worker in untaught mightiness. It teaches letting go. It teaches truly that a new line of kings is started on this earth. That is, that while the semblance of governments by crazy and fashion-loving potentates is going on, a mysterious crew of people, represented by those mentioned in this chapter, are undermining the whole business. So much for the whole world's state. As to each individual, let us know that the world's committee on Bible apologues could not have selected this particular section for this week if each of us had not had to be positively informed this week that our outward shaking circumstances are nothing, and will wage nothing to our hurt, though they may seem to keep on for a while longer. The great reign of a prospering destiny has struck its base in us because we have acknowledged that our own soul is the omnipotent Jesus Christ. This is turning toward Bethlehem. Nothing of our former photographic, stalwart stories are now acceptable.

Micah prophesied how wonderful the strength of dropping the past in Chapter V, verse 2: "Thou, Bethlehem, Ephratah, though thou be little among the thousands, yet out of thee shall he come forth unto me that is to be ruler."

We know very well how the churches and Sunday school teachers will see this section, but they have had their reiterated interpretations these many generations, and they have had as a result the present civilization. These new interpretations are rising out of the ashes of the old ones with their deathless vigors as unweakened as when the creative word first sprinkled eternity with suns to make time. Oriental books teach having the self become nothing — pure nothing — that the Self may be all, by saying: "Let not the self hide the Self." But though history cannot put her finger back to a star that tells when man first taught himself that sentence, still, shall this Samuel story quiver and quicken as a wondrously original life-breathing way to tell man of himself.

Inter-Ocean Newspaper, December 1, 1895

LESSON X

Missing

LESSON XI

The Third Influence

I Samuel 20:32-42

Last Sunday's golden text was very wonderful, and the principle exposed, by studying it from the standpoint of the new premises made it show up what we ought to see back of what happened in that piece meal of our life extending between Dec. 6 and 13.

As King Jehoram threatened to take off the head of Elisha the prophet if he did not prophesy good fortune for Israel; 900 B.C. so let it be known that it was the wisest and safest thing the International Committee could have done to put out a golden text, for all the world to read and ponder over, which had in it a good event for last week. This good event was like a pebble thrown into a stream. Those who were near the pebble got strong experience. Those who were farther off got lighter ones. If anybody knows the section of Bible apologues chosen for each week for the Sunday

71

meditation of a world he can easily snatch his main trend of affairs for the week.

Last week had it that whether we did one way or another would make no difference, so long as we were doing the best we could. Our best would have in it a great victory — an unexpected advantage on our side — a miraculousness is more manifest to those whose eyes are on the mysterious third presence in the universe than to those whose eyes are on material things, but the unexpected thing would be certain to come that week, whether we were materially minded or spiritually minded.

It was illustrated by David going out against Goliath, with a few sling stones and disposing of him very suddenly. David was one of the Israelites, and they were all hard pushed by Goliath. Some of them were very materially minded, but they got the benefit of David's sling stones just the same.

The golden text was: "The battle is the Lord's." It brought to closer attention than ever what a difference it makes to our lot in life to have a way of laying hold of the third presence in the universe. It brought closer than ever the possibility of miracles becoming every-day occurrences. There are some extraordinary things happening nowadays to those who have acquainted themselves with this third substance in space. So extraordinary that when they are recorded in print hardly one outside of investigators believe in them. Does anybody believe, for instance, that a large cancer disappeared from a man's ear in one night by his touching this third presence? Does anybody believe, outside of those who have got hold of some taste of its splendor, that a man's eyeballs grow anew in his head, and new sight was vouchsafed him by touching this wonderful third in life? Yet the things took place.

Faith is Not Necessary

When anyone touches this third One, always near by, he does not have to have faith. He gets what he wants whether he has faith or not. We don't have to have faith that four plus five will make nine, and neither do we have to have faith that this unidentified third will arrange matters in orderly fashion for us if we get one stroke of its feathers.

We do not have to exercise after it with our thoughts, nor strike out after it with our hands, nor cry after it with our voices, yet while doing all these ways we might get a waft from it that would do some wonderful advantage for us. The name of the stroke is David. The name of the disadvantages annulled is Goliath. The name of the advantage is "miracle," really but in that last weeks lesson it was called "battle" for a change of nomenclature.

These lessons are always divided into three parts but it is not so stated except once in a couple of years or so. Those three parts are: First, Point: second, Illustration; third, Influence. The point today is that this universe, different from body

and mind which is able to do exceeding abun-
dantly above that we can ask or even think on our
behalf, and that we can get so one with this third
presence that we are afraid of nothing and want
nothing. Paul said he was caught into this third
One, and could not sense anything in his body or
know anything with his mind, yet he heard the
unspeakable thing of it.

The illustration today is argon, oxygen, hydro-
gen. Argon is unmixable, unmarriageable,
unidentified, yet it is to it that oxygen and hydro-
gen must be submitted to perform as they ought
to. The inference is that if we seek first the kingdom of the third all things shall be added unto us
in divine and beautiful order. Jesus of Nazareth
called this immaculate third by several different
names. Finally he said that he had so eliminated
himself from body and mind and identified himself
with it, the unnamable third, that his name would
be the best name to use for it for the whole future
age.

The Egyptians called it "He." "He is by himself,
yet it is to him that everything owes existence."
We may infer that whenever anything miraculous
occurs to anybody he has hit the immaculate third
in some fashion which he does not explain. There
are people doing these things now who have lessons in which they try to explain how they hit the
"One by himself," but when they next attempt to
do something wonderful by close following of their
own explanations they cannot achieve it. There is

a lady at No. 1889 Indiana Avenue, Chicago, who has cured deafness, but she could not tell you how she did it, though she should write a ream of paper over with descriptions of mental states and bodily changes. The hearing threads which she spies for deaf ears are drawn from the unspeakable third presence in space. The book we call Bible is full of calls and pulls toward this One whose effects are miraculous. David represented one who had found it in a great degree, yet he could not explain himself so anybody could catch on to it and do the same thing he could.

Today's lesson exhibits how nature and man and machinery must whirl and whirl to carry out the smile of the Eternal Third when we have caught it.

As wood and glass make fire when the sun hits them at the proper focus, so Jonathan strengthens David, when they both see the same God. And David must be strong for he is to be king and ancestor of his kings. He had passed the unidentified Third and must take, the ways of man and nature and machinery as all working for the kingship.

Now, this week we are to see men and nature and machinery focusing themselves to force our destiny fast for us. We have a mission ahead, and great stresses and straits and pressure are urging us into it. Notice that Jonathan is the son of the retiring king, Saul. See how he loves David the onhastening king. So is the most precious gem of the departing power at this date. What is the departing power of this age? High caste. What is its most precious possession? Money. Does that mean that the new power just coming in will have the use of all the money now on this earth? How can they help having the use of all the money if they have faced the wonderful Third whose smile always gives the handling of all things unto whomsoever catches it?

Who are "they" who compose the incoming power of the new age? They are those who are watching the One of whom these lessons have been speaking. Are there many of them? An enormous number. Are they on the thrones of the world now? Not at all. They are not even known to the present thrones. Who composes the present thrones? Those who are called kings and queens, and emperors and presidents, with their lords and princes. They make up the high castes and dictate the fashion and arrange wars now exactly as they have been doing since men first bolstered them up with admiring them and believing in their superior rights.

How are those who are ordained to be kingly in reigning power, going to withdraw the admiration and bolstering-up beliefs of a whole world of people from such crazy potentates as are now in high places? This lesson shows it up that it is by the ownership of the most precious of the potentates. It is illustrated by Jonathan, the precious son of rattle-headed Saul, King of Israel, 1000 B.C., who became David's sworn and pledged ally. (I Samuel 20:32-42)

Read over and there will be some details come plainly to some people which will not be mentioned in the printing.

As wood is burned to nothingness when the sunglass touches it, so Saul's great court disappears when the sun-hot David touches it. And David is as innocent of trying to destroy Saul as the sun-glass of trying to burn the wood.

The Bible Will Always Apply to Men

How is Jonathan so attracted to David? As well ask how the daisy is so in love with the sun. Something in the new nature of the watchers of the uncontaminated Third is as full of drawing power as the loadstone. Something in David pulled on Jonathan's heart-strings. Something in the sun pulls up the daisy's face. Something in the watchers is a pulling principle, and even the money magnates should be astonished and angry about this time if this apologue has reached its last round of application to human existence.

These Bible sections are so accurately made up that they will apply to mankind as long as they breathe. We might take the story of Solon, Napoleon, the Prince of Wales, or any other human picture and work out a likeness for our own life, but it would only be strong and apropo if we were strong and focusing in our quality, or if a few determined and well-elected men had selected it to be read up and explained for a whole world.

There is nothing objectionable in these lessons. The men did very well to choose David with his touch of the all-conquering Third Presence instead of the Prince of Wales with his touch of dock-tailed horses for this present generation's next inspirations.

The Bible is rich with magical movements. It cannot be read without breathing forth a wind from the magical mountains. How straight the breath, and how great the miracle, when millions on millions are contemplating the same text at the same moment!

Think of the countless thousands reading today's golden text: "There is a friend that sticketh closer than a brother." Think of how many ways the text is being regarded. Some say it means a dear friend who can do like Jonathan for David. Some say it means Jesus of Nazareth who went about doing good and telling how to get free from the burning lake God his Father had prepared for us.

Some say that it means this everlasting substance that is not body and is not mind but is so different from body and mind that it is unspeakable by them. It sticketh so close that nobody ever yet got away from it. It is so friendly that whatsoever things we need we can get from it when we are submitted to its focus as sun-glass and wood to sunshine.

Today's lesson emphasizes the Emersonian theorem that the beneficent tendency streaming through all actions is forcing us all to our places. David was thrust into the very fields to hide from the anger and disgust of Saul. This caused Jonathan to see his father, Saul, in a new light, and also disgusted the nation with its ruler.

So the very stress and strains of those who are looking soulward draws attention to the incompetence of the powers that be, in some way. There is a drawing power in them which could not exhibit itself except through certain straits (verse 41). See how David's straits drew Jonathan closer (verse 42); but Jonathan, who is the worlds most precious possession could not wholly belong to David until David stood superior to him, so mind and body must be lost to need of goods before goods are wholly owned.

There is a perfect unity in the higher principles. See how Jesus taught that he who would save his life must lose it. See how Paul said that his body was dead to sensation and his mind was lost to intelligence before he caught the unspeakable. So, here too, there is a transcended state, which sometimes comes through grief itself, which teaches the Third One by himself, to whom all things owe existence.

There is But One Reality

There is no reality in a body that can lose itself; no reality in a mind that can be lost. The only reality is that One here present who cannot be lost; who is always sticking closer than a brother, whom to know is to be like. Mind can talk of spirit until it is quite heavenly and radiant; but it is now plainly demonstrated that spiritually minded people are not morally reliable people. The Third Presence is not spirit. Spirit is mind in an attenuated condition. This Third Presence is a substance which has but one name that can bring it to tangible ways, and that name confers moral integrity.

It is too late to urge that name of the Third Presence. The Impetus of demonstration is on, and it is best now to say little, and write little, think little. As a chemist holds his breath while some mighty transformation is taking place in his jars, so we hold still while the moral-integrity name of the Third One is chemicalizing earth as a whole and man as an individual.

The name of God applied to it makes man severe, domineering, and unreliable. The name is an immaculate concept. It has no power to throw off the contamination of personal opinions. This other name is immaculate. It has no power to throw off personal opinions when repeated. Who can tell whether Jesus Christ ever lived or not? He is immaculate of your mental knowledge. Who can tell whether Jesus Christ is a man or a principle, or neither? He is immaculate of such explanation. Who can tell how the name comes to have such dynamitic force? It is immaculate of history. It is unspeakable in substance and efficacy.

David said: "I come unto thee in the name." He has been praised for slinging pebbles. He had a name which trashed everything out of his way to give free transit toward his own throne. Jesus was not praised for preaching like a Beecher nor for healing like a Schlatter; was he hosannaed for knowing a name. He had faced the Third Substance in space until he was it. So his name was it. When the heavens bent, and the earth shook, and man moved in word and peace to seat him on its throne, so that any easy way to let go of body and mind might be actual for all mankind. Whoever calls the wonderful Third One here present by that name sees how people and nature and mechanics all bend and break and turn and transform to stop hope, stop sensation, stop everything that authoritative divinity may get its throne.

In the measure of each, this week, everybody sees his environmental handling him Saul's precious son. Read this lesson over more than once if you have not caught what comes freely this week and foreruns the springing forth of the unspeakable sense of authority hidden within your being.

Inter-Ocean Newspaper, December 15, 1895

LESSON XII

Doctrine Of The Holy Land

Luke 2:8-9

Before Christian reckoning of A.D. in the month of December in the city of Bethlehem, in Judea, a peasant woman gave birth to a child which she called Jesus. "And there were in the same country shepherds abiding in the field, keeping watch over their flock by night, and to an angel of the Lord came upon them, and the glory of the Lord shone around them, and they were sore afraid." (Luke 2:8-9)

This child grew to manhood taking notice of two things, namely, that the psalms and hymns he had recited in the synagogues taught that prospering power always lies along the line of moral integrity, compassion, benevolence; while daily experience proved that prospering power lies always in the line of brainy syndicating, sharp cornering of produce, and ears deaf to worthy entreaties.

Socrates, several hundred years before Jesus, had observed the same thing. Upon being asked, what was the greatest trial of the upright, he answered: "The prosperity of the wicked." Members of the great churches of modern times have noted the same thing. The New York Independent of Dec. 12, 1895, admits that the church now "tries to get rich members, and be strong in society."

It is not at all likely that those shepherds who spent their whole time on the hills watching cattle and stars had had any opportunity to take notice of the seeming discrepancy between religious assurance and practical experiences. This accounts for their glorying and singing so joyously after "all the things that they had heard and seen, as it was told them." (Verse 20) Sometimes ignorance is a good thing. "I never knew you," is a good way to deal with disease, misfortune, failure. This latter is Christian science practice. Therefore the genuine Christian Scientists of this day are the people whom the shepherds of this lesson antedated.

Genuine Christian Scientists do not find flaws in each other. They are too busy watching stars and flocks. They know nothing of the wickedness that troubles the Socratic minds of this age. They go so far as not to know even the world's diseases and pains. We can, then, easily pick out the shepherds of this date.

They rejoice in every dream prophetic of good. They sing with glee if a sick man says he can drink coffee. They shout on platforms with inspiring voices if a Presbyterian newspaper admits that "they have made a few cures of nervous disorders and are, on the whole, a conscientious sect." Every little thing fills them with fervor and expectation. If we did not appreciate that they are a perpetual "treatment" to the age we should certainly be tempted to declare that they live in the "fool's paradise," for it does not really seem, half witted to be as ticked over such babyish exhibitions of divine providence as satisfy them.

Awake to Both Sides of the Question

Now the Jesus man stands widely awake to the two sides of the question. He understands the value of knowing nothing, praising slight tokens, and he knows exactly how much headway the know-nothing make as dwellers in simple light against the syndicates, merchants, combines, cornerers of bread, etc. He sees them as balance to the darknesses which Socrates called prosperity of wickedness. He knows very well they do hold their own. He knows very well it is a third, unmixed wisdom which must seize the so-called darkness of prospering greed on the left hand and ecstatic know-nothingness called light on the right hand, and throttle them both out of existence in the twinkling of an eye to establish the new kingdom whose inhabitants are not happy because they are such fools nor prosperous because they are so smart.

Where have the preachers of Jesus Christ been tarrying that they have not spoken boldly of that land that lieth here between the prospering smartness and silly praise? What is the country that peasant woman's child discovered, stepped into, and told all the people on this earth, bad and good, black and white to step into with him and be kept unspotted thenceforth from neck and neck hustling on the one hand and undesirable inanity on the other.

It is a real country. When anybody says it is a state of mind and rolls up his eyeballs toward it as he speaks of a state of a mind, if you have even the slightest wittedness about you, you will try to remind him that every state of mind produces its own environment. Then he may possibly see that the highest states of mind should open our eyes to the sight of a country where the blessedness of life should not be always put off to some future event, when somebody's coming should do something to help the prisoners behind the bars of perhaps nineteen hundred years from now, and stop the clutch of the rich on the breath of the poor a thousand years from today, maybe.

It is only shepherds we sing and screech over a promised benefit to humanity. The Jesus Christ man says: "Step into this safe land today. If I don't have a message about how to save you now out of the bitterness of the world on the left hand, and the silliness of the shepherds on the other, I am either as silly as a shepherd or as tricky as a Gould."

Whoever repeats the name Jesus Christ and tries to explain it contaminates by the idea of materiality and sense life on the one side, or by spirituality and mental fancy on the other. Whoever lets the name convey its own potentiality finds it cutting off ideal optimism with equal severity to its cutting off sensual tendencies. It is a name which refuses to be identified. The paradise of dukes is their state of mind. The two paradises are very dissimilar. But neither one is the country where Jesus Christ walks.

To See with the Eye of Understanding

Today's Bible lesson tells of the Jesus Christ country. It is here. Whoever understands Luke sees into the country and feels the windy glory of ability to help me out of prison if I am in a stone one, is either a shepherd or a worldling. Whoever does not feel his feet swift with strength to unloose those Armenian prisoners of English and Russian gold is either a philosopher or a church pietist.

Whoever does not know how to lift up the head of bereavement and show sufficient restoration to be actual comfort, is either a thinker or an optimist.

He may have heard about a man, "Jesus who satisfied the wrath of God," or a "Christ principle of which Jesus was an expression," but he knows not the first item about Jesus Christ, that one that dwelleth in this country that is not Christ principle and is not a caterer to the world's passion for hurting innocent and helpless creatures. The name Jesus Christ has the mysterious power of showing up to the plain gaze of all people that neither silly optimism — nor world catering as identified with this birth of Jesus Christ on this earth. It soon exposes the fact that here is a land all unmixed with shepherds and philosophizers into which mankind are invited to step and lead the new life of salvation from the world the flesh and the devil; or independent of the present environment, the present unreliable body and all forms of travail of mind through matter.

The worldly wise would make even the great God himself a striver to get somewhere and do something; and they make him out a very unsuccessful striver at that. This doctrine of an unsuccessful God, agonizing along through the ages to make man behave himself, has seen the bottom plank and entire cause of all the travail of human existence.

Conditions always have their causation in beliefs. Whatsoever principle a nation holds we shall soon see how all its people experience it. If they believe there are microbes in railway coach cushions, very soon they will have diphtheria or fever. If they never heard of such notions they will keep well. So if prominent religionists insist that "God desires to save all men, but the bad must reform themselves or perish" — as the greatest religious journal of the United States declared a few weeks ago, we shall have to go on seeing mighty efforts to establish the good on earth with very little achievement.

We shall see promising, and promising, and promising of some power to be manifested by the good some time ahead, but no special present performance thereof; and no promising on the part of evil, but prompt executiveness thereof. This is travail. And it brings forth little signs of good now and then. Through the clash and clang of the battle field the slaves got free. This was the travail of good through evil. The slight freedom they got had promise in it of greater freedom. So this little signal is hailed with songs of joy and praise.

Catering to the Notions of the World

But who shall say how easy might have been the birth of freedom for the blacks if as a people we had ceased to think of God the good as so inefficient and slow, needing to crush and torture so many before he could accomplish anything? Is there not some one with rich, strong knowledge within him that it is only catering to the world-notion that hurting something is godlike which keeps hurting going on, on this earth?

This lesson speaks of angels. They are the true songs of mankind formulated. They are songs which tell of the easy triumph of peace on earth. They are men's songs about the chord of good will that stretches itself through all men alike. Why are the formulated songs of men about what has already shown itself out as accomplished and finished in the heavenly land that presses itself against us this minute, as we hide it by telling what it is going to do and how hard it is now trying to do something? "I am the door," said Jesus. "We look for a door," say the philosophers. "I am the bread," said Jesus. "We look for a way to make our living," say all the people. "Lo! I am with you alway," said Jesus. "We are on our journey heavenward, where Jesus dwells," say the religionists. "The kingdom of heaven is come," said Jesus. "It is nigh." "The kingdom of heaven is at hand." "The Father is in me." "In my Father's house are many mansions."

These texts are true. The doctrine of the heavenly land as a little thing in a manger with oxen, as going to do something for humanity in ages to come, is a universally accepted principle, but it is not Jesus Christ. That name stands for a land and friend here is in our midst, not identified with the future and independent of the past.

There was a child born who forced his eyes to see and his feet to touch that land while yet he saw how it was with the idealists and the worldlings. And that child so identified himself with that land that he was all it. His very name became its name. With one foot on idealism and one foot on worldly ways he made them both nothing — entirely nothing; to himself, and as identified with the land where there is neither bond nor free, thinking Greek nor silly barbarian, he stands now a willing door, an easy entrance, for all of us into that country.

Now suppose this were not already true, but suppose we were all educated to know about the formulating power of principles — how that we experience whatever we believe in — would it not be better to believe this new way than to believe in a struggling, striving, un-accomplishing God, and a suffering, travailing humanity? But it is true. That is exactly what this Luke 2, means for anybody who does not bring the contamination of his own notions to the story, but, instead, lets the story tell its own meaning.

Already in the Revolution

According to this meaning, we are already in the revolution prophesied by sages and saints, but it is a bloodless revolution, a painless turning over of all these hitherto invisible things into our sight. Somebody publishes it. (Verse 17) But the great receptive, gracious multitude of people, silently embrace it and live with it as Mary, the Mother. (Verse 19) We know how the kingdoms of this world are promised to become the kingdoms of our Lord Jesus Christ. Now, idealism, which rejoices over the triumph of every little bit of good, and sings about how powerful and triumphant the good is going to prove itself by and by, and worldly scheming, which laughs at such untriumphing nonsense, are the kingdoms on this globe. But they both get lost into the unmixed kingdom that lieth four-squares in our midst. And this is not the triumph of the evil, but the swallowing up of them both. Neither the other, they never will, for they are only balances on a globe of balances. They each have their ideas of Jesus Christ, but Jesus Christ is not at all like the descriptions of either one. Jesus Christ is immaculate of either the struggling good or the striding evil. There is neither male nor female in Jesus Christ, but the unidentified. One who is a whole kingdom in itself here in our midst, entered by one man whose name is the name at its doorway, "I am the door."

There are many doctrines, but they make no headway in a world of balancing; how could they? This Jesus Christ is not a doctrine. It is the living land in our midst. Here in this land, upon which our feet this moment step, there is neither love nor hate, but that third unopposed sweetness called heavenly home.

> "For oh! 'tis love, 'tis love they say,
>   That makes the world go round."

But just as much of our activity is hate while we believe in triumph of good over evil or of evil over good. There is something more wonderful than love whose mission is to balance hate. There was no child like Jesus on the earth when he came so there is no teaching of this land which swallows up both love and hate on this earth when this week's interpretations springs its green fields and homey rooftrees into view.

The New Jerusalem Is Visible

The crumbling walls of old Jerusalem make rents through which the New Jerusalem is visible. As Joshua on his seventh day's journey around Jericho cried "Shout! for the city is ours!" so all the multitudes of men may shout now, for the undescribed home they belong in is plainly in sight.

As they called Jesus a new man come among them, though he himself said he had always existed, so we speak of this land that now gives its sweet breath for our life as a New Jerusalem, while yet it is the everlasting kingdom which never can perish.

As they spoke of the heavenly visitor as a babe in a manger among the unknown peasantry, so they speak of this Jesus Christ kingdom as idealism cheaper than rags, unpractical today, but doubtless true in some golden age to come.

Fortunately it is too late for any explanations to stay its on-hastening splendor. The sweep of the centuries has ended. The word of opposition has no potency. Somebody proclaims that the New Jerusalem is here, and swings aside the curtains of common air to show its porticoes, and in the hearts of millions there is an unconquerable certainty that something has happened which means liberty from earth. That liberty from earth is what "Savior" means. There is no other safety except safety from earth.

The New York Independent explains these texts differently. It says that "in a manger" means "in a little low trough." "Swaddling clothes" are "narrow bands of cloth." "In the same country" means "in the pasture." And so on. This may feed some people as wise and complicated translations for religious bread, but those very interpretations are truly the straw bedding with which they are trying to comfort the mother multitudes who are so aware of the wonderful thing that has now happened that they do not even criticize the straw.

Something has happened. Far and near there is a great change felt. The unprecedented has begun to exhibit its undescribed ways.

"He swalloweth up death in victory, and the rebuke of his people taketh utterly away from off all the earth." The golden text is: "Behold, I bring you good tidings of great joy." There is no good tidings save only that the home we came from now shines in sight.

Inter-Ocean Newspaper, December 22, 1895

LESSON XIII

Review

The golden text of this week is: "Thy kingdom come." The moment anybody repeats that text he opens the way for his strongest characteristic to get a new grip on his affairs.

For anybody's strongest characteristic is the ruler. Even if he keeps his jealousy out of sight, he is being slyly run by it if it is his hardest trait. There is a mental chemistry with which a strong trait can be neutralized and another force takes its place. Then if anybody prays, "Thy kingdom come," why, the new force will respond.

Today's Bible lesson intimates that some new force has been invited to reign over each of us and we shall certainly feel its influence the coming week. The last year's Bible readings have certainly exposed things which no religion in this world had brought to light till they came out. They have asked only one thing of us as we have read them, and that has been, "Bring no preconceived notions." Even a rose will whisper new stories to an unprejudiced ear and eye. What then, shall not the rose-bloom of ancient inspiration whisper to an unconverted reader?

This last year's Bible segments were chosen by a committee of men who were choicest treasures of many church congregations. So there has been a choice flavor about every lesson, and that flavor has helped the subtle nourishment it has contained to sift its substance through the mentality of even those people who never read it either in Sunday school or out.

These lessons have been revolutionary. They have shown that that unconverted streak in all human beings which they have fought with and called Satan was their Jesus Christ nature. It is that which is never married, when you pledge yourself, and is never interested in your most exciting business schemes. It is that which prods you on and makes you so restless. It is that which stares with its mysterious objection while you are shooting birds or catching fish. That is the Jesus Christ in man.

Its eternal message is: "My kingdom is not of this world." You cannot be so good as to please it; you cannot be so bad as to drown it. Neither goodness nor badness interests it. Its kingdom is the mystic Third — non-identified, non- partial. These lessons have exposed the fact that all religions have had for their mission the re-enforcement of the balance of good against the evil on this earth. They have had to rouse themselves up every now and then with some new statements applicable to the age which needed an impetus in order to keep the two kingdoms, good and bad, evenly balanced. The good has always had to struggle and fight and starve and agonize in order to lift up its head, while the evil has just stridden in splendid ease, without effort. The two kingdoms of struggle and ease were only the principles of balance. Night and day, peace and war, life and death, health and disease, spirit and matter. These are the kingdoms of this world, always reposing in even balance.

Swallowing Energy's Blind Force

These are the two kingdoms which are to be swallowed up in the third unidentified, unthinkable One. As the attention of a globe has been turned to the mysterious Third by these lessons, there is some reference to it now, when we repeat the golden text: "Thy kingdom come."

Whoever has his attention turned toward that prodding, unconverted streak within himself, and calls it Jesus Christ, and says "Thy kingdom come," is soon startled at the changes that transpire in his life. He may be as bad as he was before, but his goodness counts for nothing. He gets the promise: "The righteousness of the righteous shall not save him."

Slowly, may be, but surely, indeed, he feels the mysterious suction of some swallowing energy. He understands the promises: "He will swallow up death in victory . . ." "He will take possession of the righteous." Nothing counts as it did before he acknowledged that his unconverted, unmarried, uninterested streak was his Jesus Christ chord. Jonathan Edwards fought with this streak till he fainted away on the banks of the Connecticut River, but he never conquered it. He called it the devil.

These lessons have named it by another name which they have frankly explained was not its final name, but its introductory name.

These lessons have shown that it was not because David was skillful at slinging pebbles that he hit Goliath so shrewdly, but because he had paid attention to that perpetually present chord in himself, and had a name for it.

"Thou comest to me with sword and with a spear, and with a shield, but I come to thee in the name of the Lord." There were thousands of Jews in his day who could sling stones as well as he could, but they were not attentive to the secret chord. We read of how seven hundred left-handed Benjaminites could sling at a hair's breadth and not miss, but they never succeeded in an encounter with their special Goliath, because they neither notice nor fought with the unconquered One within them. It is very strengthening to fight with the unconquerable. Notice how it revived up that old piece of rags and scorn, called Job; to run to the right hand and to the left, forward and back, to contend with the Almighty.

The Kingdom of the Unconverted

This week some strength like the unconquerable chord shall manifest itself. The deathless health, the unkillable fire of fervor the new breath with reviving, shall come on.

These powers have nothing in common with common health, which can hide itself; with common prosperity, which can get knocked over with common breathing, which can stop; but they shall come from that unidentified everlasting enemy to good and evil — the mysterious kingdom of the unconverted Third. "My kingdom is an everlasting kingdom, not of this world." Moses called it the "I Am." He watched it so faithfully that it spread itself as a pillar of fire by night and a cloud by day, to guide him and the 2,000,000 Israelites running away from Pharaoh.

But he got to watching Hobab; the son of Raguel, and praising him as an excellent guide and so forgot the all-conquering, unerring pillar of fire. This kept him prowling around and around in the desert for forty years.

David was one step ahead of Moses, for he would not use Saul's shield and armor when he was setting forth against Goliath. So he succeeded. Hobab and Saul's armor are different names for the same principle.

As Charles Dickens always introduced us to the same characters in every book, dressing them in slightly different clothes and varying their conversations a little so the Bible keeps presenting the same profound fact of our life. The sweet fact that we may count on the support and victoriousness of our Almighty I Am — the uninterested streak within — if we notice it. No need to praise it. No need to scold it. Give it attention. That sets its action going, and the kingdoms of our — what? The New Testament calls it Lord Jesus Christ. The Old Testament calls it Lord. This golden text calls it "thy kingdom."

Complaints of Gideon and Naomi

Saul had all his attention focused on Samuel, a man like himself. Feeling the protesting chord within he tried to break away from Samuel's influence. Not having his eye trained, or even turned toward the conquering chord, which stretches itself to all alike, he lost his wits and his strength. By being away from Samuel, he initiated Moses in his act of drawing away his attention from the guiding I Am.

Gideon quarreled and argued with this all-conquering kingdom, and even that way of dealing was better than nothing for with its victorious mightiness he took 800 men and overthrew 135,000 Midianites.

Naomi kept her eye on it, and whined and howled before it till it thrilled beautiful Ruth to defend and preserve her. Take notice that Naomi did her lamenting before this Lord, the unmanageable something that strings its eternal presence through all alike. She did not complain of people, but of the Lord, and to the Lord.

"The Lord hath dealt very bitterly with me." Some books have urged praise of this Lord, because their writers discovered that something new defended them when they praised it.

But if they had complained unto it and kept silence before their neighbors, this Lord would have defended them just the same. Naomi taught this. The story of Naomi is meant to teach this. This Lord chord is too majestic to be cajoled by praise, and too glorious to be injured by blame.

Eli and his sons were putting into the amber of narrative to show that scientific assurances of good on the right hand are to be balanced by dissolutions of evil on the left hand, or evil will get to adopting the affirmations all to itself. As, if a man says, "All is good," he will find pain and poverty and sickness confronting him in full measure to swallow his affirmation.

Out of affirmations unbalanced by denials has grown that proposition that pain is remedial. Also that we learn by defeats and afflictions. Such proclamations keep pain, defeat, poverty, affliction, in plain sight. All the people who call pain good, and say that their misfortunes have taught them wisdom are wimpy and draggled in general appearance; white faced, and sanctimonious; also exceedingly self-righteous.

Close of the Review of the Year

Samuel was made a figurehead to show through all time that a positive mind projecting thoughts is not a desirable machine. It is true that the projective and positive minds do bring things to pass to suit themselves up to a certain point, but finally their mental machinery gets worn out and those whom they have bolstered up or governed go all to pieces.

It is far better to be like Jesus and mind our own business. This is done best by letting the wonderful kingdom that is already here in our midst show itself, instead of graving it all over with our "missions of reforming the world." "Thou shalt not make unto thee any graven image or likeness."

Goliath was pictured on the pages of sacred instruction to show how easily we are expected to erase the sum total of hardship and horror called our human lot or environment. We have a name for the secret power within us which will guide even a sling-stone aright if we repeat it. Nobody is urged to repeat this name, but that extensive work on magic handled so carelessly by Christendom has proclaimed that "in that name many wonderful works shall be done."

Thus closes this year's review by names, events, religious teachings. We do not go forward into a kingdom.

The kingdom comes. On our enraptured sight its miraculous towers and mosques and rooftrees burst. It is the home of our ever protesting Lord chord.

Attention to this one has given unto its kingdom all our mind and body. If any student of Bible stories makes them tell any less than this he cuts under and limits their meanings, and, of course, must have a life cut under and limited.

It is the matchless ministry of Jesus Christ which saith: "I set before you an open door which no man can shut."

It is not true that these renderings of Bible stories are incontrovertible? Thus they are the opening of the unshuttable door.

> "O airs from the hills of glory blow!
> O Life from the swells of the infinite flow!
> Let thy peace, my father, descend upon me;
> Let thy peace, my father, the world see."

Inter-Ocean Newspaper, December 29, 1895

Notes

Other Books by Emma Curtis Hopkins

- *Class Lessons of 1888 (WiseWoman Press)*
- *Bible Interpretations (WiseWoman Press)*
- *Esoteric Philosophy in Spiritual Science (WiseWoman Press)*
- *Genesis Series 1894 (WiseWoman Press)*
- *High Mysticism (WiseWoman Press)*
- *Self Treatments with Radiant I Am (WiseWoman Press)*
- *The Gospel Series (WiseWoman Press)*
- *Judgment Series in Spiritual Science (WiseWoman Press)*
- *Drops of Gold (WiseWoman Press)*
- *Resume (WiseWoman Press)*
- *Scientific Christian Mental Practice (DeVorss)*

Books about Emma Curtis Hopkins and her teachings

- *Emma Curtis Hopkins, Forgotten Founder of New Thought – Gail Harley*
- *Unveiling Your Hidden Power: Emma Curtis Hopkins' Metaphysics for the 21st Century (also as a Workbook and as A Guide for Teachers) – Ruth L. Miller*
- *Power to Heal: Easy reading biography for all ages –Ruth Miller*

To find more of Emma's work, including some previously unpublished material, log on to:

www.highwatch.org

www.emmacurtishopkins.com

WISEWOMAN PRESS

Vancouver, WA 98665
800.603.3005
www.wisewomanpress.com

Books by Emma Curtis Hopkins

- *Resume*
- *The Gospel Series*
- *Class Lessons of 1888*
- *Self Treatments including Radiant I Am*
- *High Mysticism*
- *Genesis Series 1894*
- *Esoteric Philosophy in Spiritual Science*
- *Drops of Gold Journal*
- *Judgment Series*
- *Bible Interpretations: Series I, thru XXII*

Books by Ruth L. Miller

- *Unveiling Your Hidden Power: Emma Curtis Hopkins' Metaphysics for the 21st Century*
- *Coming into Freedom: Emily Cady's Lessons in Truth for the 21st Century*
- *150 Years of Healing: The Founders and Science of New Thought*
- *Power Beyond Magic: Ernest Holmes Biography*
- *Power to Heal: Emma Curtis Hopkins Biography*
- *The Power of Unity: Charles Fillmore Biography*
- *Power of Thought: Phineas P. Quimby Biography*
- *The Power of Insight: Thomas Troward Biography*
- *The Power of the Self: Ralph Waldo Emerson Biography*
- *Uncommon Prayer*
- *Spiritual Success*
- *Finding the Path*

Books by Ute Maria Cedilla

- *The Mysticism of Emma Curtis Hopkins*
- *Volume 1 Finding the Christ*
- *Volume 2 Ministry: Realizing The Christ One in All*

List of
Bible Interpretation Series
with dates from 1st to 22nd Series.

This list is for the 1st to the 22nd Series. Emma produced twenty eight Series of Bible Interpretations.

She followed the Bible Passages provided by the International Committee of Clerics who produced the Bible Quotations for each year's use in churches all over the world.

Emma used these for her column of Bible Interpretations in both the Christian Science Magazine, at her Seminary and in the Chicago Inter-Ocean Newspaper.

First Series

July 5 - September 27, 1891

Lesson 1	The Word Made Flesh	July 5th
	John 1:1-18	
Lesson 2	Christ's First Disciples	July 12th
	John 1:29-42	
Lesson 3	All Is Divine Order	July 19th
	*John 2:1-1*1 (Christ's first Miracle)	
Lesson 4	Jesus Christ and Nicodemus	July 26th
	John 3:1-17	
Lesson 5	Christ at Samaria	August 2nd
	John 4:5-26 (Christ at Jacob's Well)	
Lesson 6	Self-condemnation	August 9th
	John 5:17-30 (Christ's Authority)	
Lesson 7	Feeding the Starving	August 16th
	John 6:1-14 (The Five Thousand Fed)	
Lesson 8	The Bread of Life	August 23rd
	John 6:26-40 (Christ the Bread of Life)	
Lesson 9	The Chief Thought	August 30th
	John 7:31-34 (Christ at the Feast)	
Lesson 10	Continue the Work	September 6th
	John 8:31-47	
Lesson 11	Inheritance of Sin	September 13th
	John 9:1-11, 35-38 (Christ and the Blind Man)	
Lesson 12	The Real Kingdom	September 20th
	John 10:1-16 (Christ the Good Shepherd)	
Lesson 13	In Retrospection	September 27th
	Review	

Second Series

October 4 - December 27, 1891

Lesson 1	Mary and Martha *John 11:21-44*	October 4th
Lesson 2	Glory of Christ *John 12:20-36*	October 11th
Lesson 3	Good in Sacrifice *John 13:1-17*	October 18th
Lesson 4	Power of the Mind *John 14:13; 15-27*	October 25th
Lesson 5	Vines and Branches *John 15:1-16*	November 1st
Lesson 6	Your Idea of God *John 16:1-15*	November 8th
Lesson 7	Magic of His Name *John 17:1-19*	November 15th
Lesson 8	Jesus and Judas *John 18:1-13*	November 22nd
Lesson 9	Scourge of Tongues *John 19:1-16*	November 29th
Lesson 10	Simplicity of Faith *John 19:17-30*	December 6th
Lesson 11	Christ is All in All *John 20: 1-18*	December 13th
Lesson 12	Risen With Christ *John 21:1-14*	December 20th
Lesson 13	The Spirit is Able Review of Year	December 27th

Third Series

Fourth Series

April 3 - June 26, 1892

Fifth Series

Sixth Series

Seventh Series

January 1 - March 31, 1893

Eighth Series

April 2 - June 25, 1893

Ninth Series

Tenth Series

Eleventh Series

January 1 – March 25, 1894

Twelfth Series

April 1 – June 24, 1894

120

Thirteenth Series

July 1 – September 30, 1894

Lesson 1	The Birth of Jesus *Luke 2:1-16*	July 1st
Lesson 2	Presentation in the Temple *Luke 2:25-38*	July 8th
Lesson 3	Visit of the Wise Men *Matthew 1:2-12*	July 15th
Lesson 4	Flight Into Egypt *Mathew 2:13-23*	July 22nd
Lesson 5	The Youth of Jesus *Luke2:40-52*	July 29th
Lesson 6	The "All is God" Doctrine *Luke 2:40-52*	August 5th
Lesson 7	Missing	August 12th
Lesson 8	First Disciples of Jesus *John 1:36-49*	August 19th
Lesson 9	The First Miracle of Jesus *John 2:1-11*	August 26th
Lesson 10	Jesus Cleansing the Temple *John 2:13-25*	September 2nd
Lesson 11	Jesus and Nicodemus *John 3:1-16*	September 9th
Lesson 12	Jesus at Jacob's Well *John 4:9-26*	September 16th
Lesson 13	Daniel's Abstinence *Daniel 1:8-20*	September 23rd
Lesson 14	Review *John 2:13-25*	September 30th

Fourteenth Series

Fifteenth Series

January 6-March 31, 1895

Sixteenth Series

April 7-June 30, 1895

Seventeenth Series

July 7 – September 29, 1895

Lesson 1	The Bread of Energy *Exodus 22:1-17*	July 7th
Lesson 2	Grandeur is Messiahship *Exodus 32:30-35*	July 14th
Lesson 3	Temperance *Leviticus 10:1-9*	July 21st
Lesson 4	The Alluring Heart of Man *Numbers 10:29-36*	July 28th
Lesson 5	As a Man Thinketh Numbers 13:17-23	August 4th
Lesson 6	Rock of Eternal Security *Numbers 31:4-9*	August 11th
Lesson 7	Something Behind *Deuteronomy 6:3-15*	August 18th
Lesson 8	What You See Is What You Get *Joshua 3:5-17*	August 25th
Lesson 9	Every Man To His Miracle *Joshua 6:8-20*	September 1st
Lesson 10	Every Man To His Harvest *Joshua 14:5-14*	September 8th
Lesson 11	Every Man To His Refuge *Joshua 20:1-9*	September 15th
Lesson 12	The Twelve Propositions Joshua 24:14-25	September 22nd
Lesson 13	Review I Kings 8:56	September 29th

125

Eighteenth Series

Oct 6 – December 29, 1895

Lesson 1	Missing	October 6th
Lesson 2	Gideon's Triumph *Judges 7:13-23*	October 13th
Lesson 3	The Divine Ego *Ruth 1:4-22*	October 20th
Lesson 4	All is Good *I Samuel 3:1-11*	October 27th
Lesson 5	If Thine Eye Be Single *I Samuel 7:5-12*	November 3rd
Lesson 6	Saul Chosen King *I Samuel 10:17-27*	November 10th
Lesson 7	Saul Rejected *I Samuel 15:10-23*	November 17th
Lesson 8	Temperance *Isaiah 5:11*	November 24th
Lesson 9	The Lord Looketh Upon the Heart *I Samuel 16:1-13*	December 1st
Lesson 10	Missing	December 8th
Lesson 11	The Third Influence *I Samuel 20:32-42*	December 15th
Lesson 12	The Doctrine of the Holy Land *Luke 2:8-9*	December 22nd
Lesson 13	Review	December 29th

126

Nineteenth Series

January 5 – March 29, 1896

Lesson 1	Missing	January 5th
Lesson 2	Missing	January 12th
Lesson 3	Lesson on Repentance *Luke 3:15-22*	January 19th
Lesson 4	"The Early Ministry of Jesus" *Luke 4:22*	January 26th
Lesson 5	Missing	February 2nd
Lesson 6	Missing	February 9th
Lesson 7	The Secret Note *Luke 6:41-49*	February 16th
Lesson 8	Answered Prayer *Luke 6:41-49*	February 23rd
Lesson 9	Letting Go The Old Self *Luke 9:18-27*	March 1st
Lesson 10	"Me, Imperturbed" *Luke 10:25-37*	March 8th
Lesson 11	Lord's Prayer *Luke 11:1-13*	March 15th
Lesson 12	Be Not Drunk With Wine *Luke 12:37-46*	March 22nd
Lesson 13	The Winds of Living Light *Luke 12:8*	March 29th

Emma Curtis Hopkins was absent on a voyage to Vera Cruz, Mexico to bring her ill son back to the USA. She left December 28, 1895 and returned February 6, 1896. This would account for missing lessons in this quarter. She may have mailed the two in January or they may have been written previously.

Twentieth Series

Twenty-First Series

July 5 – September 27, 1896

Lesson 1	The Lord Reigneth *II Samuel 2:1-11*	July 5th
Lesson 2	Adeptship *II Samuel 5:1-12*	July 12th
Lesson 3	The Ark *II Samuel 6:1-12*	July 19th
Lesson 4	Purpose of An Adept *II Samuel 7:4-16*	July 26th
Lesson 5	Individual Emancipatioin *II Samuel 9:1-13*	August 2nd
Lesson 6	The Almighty Friend *II Samuel 10:8-19*	August 9th
Lesson 7	Salvation Is Emancipation(missing) *Psalms 32:1-1*	August 16th
Lesson 8	Individual Emancipation *II Samuel 15:1-12*	August 23rd
Lesson 9	Absalom's Defeat And Death *II Samuel 16:9-17*	August 30th
Lesson 10	The Crown Of Effort *I Chronicles 22:6-16*	September 6th
Lesson 11	"Thy Gentleness Hath Made Me Great *II Samuel 22*	September 13th
Lesson 12	A Fool For Christ's Sake *Proverbs 16:7-33*	September 20th
Lesson 13	The Lord is a Strong Tower Proverbs 28:10	September 27th

September 27 of this quarter is a Review of the International Committee listing, not Emma's usual listing and review of the previous lessons in the quarter.

Twenty-Second Series